dream, build, repeat.

HARNESS FEAR TO CONFIDENTLY PURSUE YOUR BIGGEST DREAMS

♡ Casey
Sharperson

CASEY SHARPERSON

Published by Casey Carea LLC.

Edited by ELOHAI International Publishing & Media

ISBN: 978-1-7334236-0-1

Printed in the United States of America

Dedication

Alice Carson Tisdale, Mama T., while you started out as the director of Claflin University's Honors College, you quickly became more than that to me. You said "yes" and provided me with the opportunity to be the first person admitted into the class of 2013. During a critical part of my life, you were also the one who had a conversation with me that pulled me out of a pit of despair and into purpose. You're the one who asked, "When is your book coming?" Thank you for shepherding me under your watchful and caring eye. Thank you for always believing in me. I love you.

My family – My parents, brother, and extended family, thank you for holding me accountable and praying for me along this journey. You are my rocks who consistently point me back to the truth of Christ by faith.

Author's Note

There was a point in time that I never would have shared my stories of failure. I would have hidden behind my accomplishments instead of sharing my full truth with transparency. I would have shared the flowery picture of success without addressing the trauma along the way. However, by faith, I'm sharing what it looks like to dream an impossible dream, build an epic thing, and do it all over again. My hope is that you don't judge me when you see me in the street. My other hope is that you walk away with a plan of action to get off the sidelines and into the game. The concept of *Dream, Build, Repeat* came about during a conversation with a client about the process for fearlessly, boldly, and confidently pursuing her dream. I boiled it down to three main points:

Dream – the process of identifying, discovering, and naming the dream.

Build – the activation process, and seeing the dream come to fruition.

Repeat – perseverance and diligence to continue down a path, even though it may be hard, scary, or lengthy. That's it! This process isn't meant to be cumbersome, but it *is* meant to challenge you. We're going to go "there" to ensure that you are building your big dream and not just being safe by building what makes sense.

These concepts can be applied to students, entrepreneurs, corporate leaders, and influencers of all kinds. Let's cancel limiting beliefs and replace them with actionable strategies to activate your genius and share it with your sphere of influence. Know that I'm on your side rooting for you. My inbox is always open. Let's go!

Let's Be Friends!

Tag me on social media, use the hashtag #DreamBuildRepeat and let me know your takeaways, questions, and revelations! Leave a review on Amazon and Barnes & Noble.

Purchase a copy or a few for your colleagues, friends, and organizations.

Website: www.CaseySharperson.com

Facebook: @CaseyCarea

Instagram: @CaseyCarea

Twitter: @CaseyCarea

YouTube: Casey Sharperson

Email: Hello@CaseySharperson.com

Podcast: Dream Build Repeat with Casey Sharperson

Request Me to Speak

Have a retreat, conference, podcast or corporate gathering where you want a dynamic speaker or trainer? Head over to www.CaseySharperson.com to submit a request.

Table of Contents

Part 3: Repeat

Foreword

Dreams are meant to be lived, not just longed after.

I've always believed this. But it wasn't until I started working with women that I realized we've never been taught to properly dream.

Instead, we've been taught to fantasize. To imagine. And to live in the land of "what if" and "one day."

We wait for Prince Charming to rescue us.

We wait to make sure everyone else is okay.

And, we wait for the best things in life to come to us, not through us.

That's what a lady is supposed to do right?

For some reason, we believe that dreams are something far off in the distance. A reality only experienced by those who are super blessed, chosen or lucky.

The truth is that as women, we've been conditioned to settle. And, we've been mis-taught the true purpose and power of a woman armed with a dream.

Dream, Build, Repeat.

Dreams are not designed to be fairytale filled with fluffy possibilities, but instead a roadmap to the future you desire.

Your dream should focus you and help you find the path, mentorship, community, and tools necessary to build a life that lights you up . . . and invites others around you to do the same.

One of my greatest honors is mentoring women. One of the most dynamic women I've mentored is, by far, Casey Sharperson. When we met, I was immediately impressed with her level of hunger and focus. While most of my clients were in their mid-40s to early 60s, Casey jumped in to our high-end, premium-priced mastermind while in her early 20s.

She was poised, determined, incredibly self-aware, and ready to build a legacy now.

She is what I was hoping for when I had the dream - the vision - of helping women unlock their gifts, potential, and destiny. That's the only way to awaken a new generation of women capable of finding and fulfilling the calling on their lives.

I've had a front row seat to watch Casey evolve, reinvent, launch, and lead globally. I love seeing her business flourish. I love seeing her speak around the world. But, what I love most is seeing her do the work to build her dream, activate her potential, and step into a higher dimension of leadership.

The first time we spoke five years ago, she said then that she wanted to help women step into their dreams. I remember that conversation very well. But, unlike most women, she didn't just talk about it. And, she didn't just long for it.

I'm thrilled that she's finally sharing with you what it really takes to live your dream.

Foreword

Dream Build Repeat is a manifesto for the modern day woman looking to live a life worthy of the calling she has received, while also learning how to embody an action plan that makes it happen. You see, I consider Casey a Proverbs 21:5 kind of a woman. The scripture says, "The plans of the diligent lead to profit."

Diligence requires a unique mix of intention, steadfastness, and surrender. For every woman who has been afraid to dream or felt frustrated that the dream is taking too long, Casey meets you right where you are with the inspiration and insight you've been waiting for.

So have your favorite pen and highlighters ready.

I firmly believe that this is your chance to experience a quantum shift in every area of your life. Your dream is ready to be resurrected and activated. That's why you've picked up this book. That's why you're here.

It's your time.

May you appreciate every word that follows. May you participate with the author as she takes you page-by-page into your next level of purpose. Most importantly, may you recognize the beauty and necessity of who you are and why the world needs you for such a time as this.

Agape,

Marshawn Evans Daniels
Godfidence Coach®
Reinvention Strategist for Women, Founder of SheProfits.com

Dream, Build, Repeat.

PART I

DREAM

Dream, Build, Repeat.

one

Shattered

In Topeka, Kansas, where I grew up, the people who looked like me were few and far between. I often found myself watching television shows like *Moesha, The Proud Family, Family Matters* and sitcoms with families who looked a little bit like me. I also found myself seeking after movies, books, and any semblance of similarity to my own family, which was quite different than what I usually saw around me. I found that in *The Cosby Show. The Cosby Show* was iconic. I could see a two-parent, successful family. I could look at the attorney, Clair Huxtable and a young girl, Rudy, who reminded me so much of myself. I grew attached to Vanessa, the daughter with a little bit of sass and Denise who was just a little bit different. I could see a little of myself in every single character on the screen, and one day, I finally had a chance to see him in person!

He was Dr. Heathcliff Huxtable, Claflin University's commencement speaker for the class of 1999. My cousin was graduating that year and we had just moved to South Carolina from Topeka, and when I heard that we could get tickets to see Dr. Huxtable, I was over the moon. That show was so transformational for me.

Even later in life when I found out about *A Different World* it just confirmed the fact that I really, really, really wanted to go to Hillman College. Nevertheless, I was able to sit there in that auditorium and listen to the iconic Dr. Huxtable, and it was at that moment that I said, I need to go here. I need to attend Claflin University. I was awestruck.

Claflin was significant to me because my great uncle, Nelson Brownlee, my grandfather's half-brother was the winningest women's basketball coach in the school's history. In fact, during his twenty-seven-year career, he lead the Lady Panthers to seventeen Eastern Intercollegiate Athletic Conference Tournament championships, twelve National Association of Intercollegiate Athletes (NAIA) tournament appearances, seven NAIA District VI championships, six South Eastern Athletic Conference championships, two NAIA tournament runner-up finishes and 623 victories. He was legit and a huge reason why I was drawn to the university. In fact, we were invited back several times to attend basketball games and events. By third grade, I knew that I wanted to attend an HBCU (Historically Black College and University) and I wanted to cheer. I recall seeing the cheerleaders and being shocked at how different they were from the Pop Warner, UCA Varsity style I was used to. Now, if you're new to this idea of historically black colleges and universities, you should know that they tend to have a little bit of extra flavor in everything that's done, and cheerleading was no different. Instead of sharp, stiff movements, these cheerleaders were stomping, shaking, and body rolling. Obviously, that became my next goal.

To recap, I wanted to attend Claflin because they had commencement ceremonies that were the bomb. I wanted to attend Claflin because there was an amazing cheerleading squad. I wanted to attend Claflin because I saw the most beautiful woman with this glittery sash and gorgeous crown, and she was *The* Miss Claflin University. That was the very last thing that sealed the deal for me... at nine years old.

I went on to live my life and there was a part of me that forgot about all these promises and vows that I made to myself. I forgot about all the amazing things that I would do at Claflin because there were so many other things going on like competitive cheerleading, drama, band, track, Girl Scouts, working, and everything else. Over time, I learned more about other programs and universities, and then I also became very, very passionate about leaving South Carolina. I wanted to be around different people, experiences, and cultures.

Pause and Reflect: It's interesting how little moments that some would deem insignificant have such a profound affect. Do you remember what it was like to fully commit to an idea with child-like faith?

By the end of my junior year, Claflin was no longer on my list simply because it was in South Carolina. However, through various circumstances (i.e. My parents literally threw me in the car and told me we were going for a campus visit. There may or may not have been a crying fit thrown en route, but my parents didn't play, so my fit didn't matter.) I ended up with the opportunity to apply and get accepted into Claflin University. In fact, at the time of my acceptance, I only applied to two schools, paid to take the SAT again, and had a plan of action to get into ANY school that was out of state. I'd planned on retaking the SAT to get an even higher score to gain increased access to scholarship opportunities. After all, my parents told me for years that college was my financial responsibility. It felt like the weight of the world on my seventeen-year-old shoulders. As you might imagine, I was in utter shock when right after Labor Day, I received an acceptance letter to Claflin and I had ten days to confirm if I would be attending the following fall. I later found out that I was the very first person to be accepted into the Alice Carson Tisdale Honors College at Claflin University that year.

It was a crazy and surreal experience, but I also looked at that letter and the circumstances surrounding it as confirmation that I was probably supposed to be there. I was slowly reminded about the other dreams I had as a little girl, and I began to think that every other plan and desire that I had for my time at Claflin would come to pass.

I tried out for the cheerleading squad and made it... and my second check box was complete. I continued on this path of achievement and became really involved on campus. I was named Miss Freshman as a member of the Student Government Association a few weeks after I started school. I went on to compete in various pageants and operated in different leadership roles on campus. My perfect college life started to fall into place. My sophomore year came to an end, and I had the chance to run for Miss Claflin. I thought it was a great time to run because I had plenty of time to get the title, do amazing things with it, and be a positive influence on campus and the community. However, at the same time, I was pledging Alpha Kappa Alpha Sorority Incorporated and my dad had been diagnosed with Stage IV Non-Hodgkin's Lymphoma in the beginning of that semester. A note here about Stage IV cancer: there isn't a Stage V. It was a diagnosis that none of us saw coming and one that rocked my family to the core. Every circumstance and every situation around me said, "Casey, this probably isn't the time to do it. Instead of using this as a time of distraction, really you should be focusing on other things." However, that dream and vision of becoming Miss Claflin was so present in the forefront of my mind that I decided to press through. I decided to go for it anyway.

It felt really chaotic. It felt off. I didn't have a true peace. There was a lot of anxiety surrounding the entire process during the campaign. I was also practicing for the probate show to be presented on campus as a new sorority member. It was a lot of pressure. I ran for Miss Claflin on the platform of cancer awareness also, probably not the best time, just due to the fact that everything was so fresh and unprocessed, but I went ahead with the campaign.

It was such a learning experience and there were things that I realized I could have done differently and that was that. I wasn't heartbroken, just a little disappointed when I did not win the title. The good news was that I had another year to make it happen. I was able to keep working, building relationships, while remaining active on campus. It also gave me some time to process and deal with my dad's cancer diagnosis and treatment with my family.

Pause and Reflect: Having tunnel vision towards a dream and goal is great until you lose focus of your emotional, physical, and spiritual health along the way. While the hustle at all costs mentality looks great on the outside, it's a way to ensure that you miss the mark in other important areas. Have you been guilty of getting stuck in the grind and ignoring what's equally as important?

Fast forward to the end of my junior year. I had so much peace. When the sign up for Miss Claflin came around, I was ready. I knew that this was the time. I had received so much clarity about what I wanted. I'd gotten so much clearer about my path and about the details of my platform. It focused on creating change, increasing confidence, and impacting the campus and community for the better. I wanted to encourage people and boost their self-esteem. I wanted to put Claflin on the map with different types of community service projects. I ran on this fun, unique platform that I was so passionate about and I loved it. I had a fancy acronym and everything!

As I started going through all of the steps from the preparation, to the campaign, to the pageant, the level of peace I felt throughout the entire process was vastly different. In my heart I just knew it was what I should have been doing. I felt like I was born to encourage people to aspire for more. I would finally have a larger platform to encourage my fellow students rather than having to rely on one-on-one outreach. This was ideal for me. It was finally time for the vision that I had cast back in 1999 to come into full fruition, and I was ready for it.

It was my time. I was so sure of it. This time, I prayed about it. This time, I asked God what I should do. This time, I had a coach to talk me through different speech tactics, and this time, I had a stylist. This time, I had a different hairstyle for every single outfit change on stage. This time, I had a professional makeup artist. This was my time, so I walked on that stage knowing that this title was mine. It wasn't from a perspective of entitlement, I just had a level of knowing and understanding that this was a dream and clearly God was going to give me the desires of my heart. Wasn't that my divine right? Wasn't that my choice? I deserved it.

When the curtains closed and the voting polls opened, I was pretty relaxed, but I still counted down on the clock for the results. Then, that familiar ping went off on my laptop. The results were in! My hands shook in anticipation and excitement, and I clicked the email icon. I began to scan and scroll, sifting through the results.

There they were. Right there in orange and maroon. The title of Miss Claflin University was… not me.

Shocked. I stared at the screen in utter disbelief. This was NOT happening. I am tearing up while writing this, remembering that moment when all of the air left my lungs and the room began to spin. It was as though I could feel that huge pit in my stomach again that formed when I saw another person's name next to the place I felt was mine. It felt like a horrendous nightmare. Who goes for this position twice and loses twice?

I thought back to every single person who told me that I was the right person for this position. Clearly, they all lied to me. I thought back to every step that I took to position myself well for this. All a waste of time. I thought back to every opportunity that I'd earned based on my leadership skills. None of it was enough. It didn't matter.

That pit in my stomach grew as I began to focus on every time where I had been good, but not good enough. Every time I felt like I had crushed an opportunity only to find out the people who made the decision didn't think so. Every time I was praised but didn't see that support when it counted.

"Do I even have a right to feel upset? Is that selfish? Isn't it just a title?" I began to ask myself. Surely, I couldn't share any of this with anyone. They'd just judge me and tell me to get over it. No big deal.

As I sat in my room, I could not put my many different emotions into words, but I knew I never wanted to feel this way again.

I never wanted to experience giving my all to something only for it not to work out. I never wanted to put myself in a position again to be embarrassed. I never wanted to put myself in a position where I felt like I had wasted time, resources, and energy. I never wanted to put myself and my ideas out there again. If I had just quit while I was ahead, I wouldn't have been in that position.

So that day in my dorm room of Claflin University, that dream and all the others died.

Pause and Reflect: The death of a dream is painful. The results of not pursuing a dream are riddled with frustration and confusion. You see, while the dream might not be your purpose, the dream is the path to purpose discovery. Could it be the reason that you feel lost, stuck, and misunderstood is because you placed your dream in the far corner of your heart due to fear and relieving the pain of past rejection?

It really may seem small and it may seem petty, but what happens when you're entering a season or a time of depression is that even the irrational makes complete sense. Even the idea that, "It wasn't your time," doesn't sound right. In that state, what sounded more accurate to me was that *I wasn't worthy, and nobody liked me anyway.* It seems logical to assume and to assess that you're not worthy of anything good after a major rejection. When a dream dies or a dream doesn't come to fruition in the way that you anticipate, your life stops. There are people who will press through with ease and there will be people who don't. I didn't. In fact, I was so broken and so distraught that I didn't leave my room for three days. I didn't eat. I didn't watch television. I didn't do anything but cry and stare at those painted cinder block walls. The only reason that I answered the phone or responded to texts is because I thought that people would show up and look for me, and I really did not want to have a conversation with anyone. I remember my parents calling to check up on me, and I didn't tell them how I was feeling because again, it was embarrassing. How could I tell people that I'm upset about not placing in a pageant? Even though for me, it was less about the title and more about my purpose. It was about how I already encouraged people around campus, and the title would help me do it in a bigger and better way. I wanted everyone to know that they could do something different and stand out as leaders in the community. I wanted them to know their voices were important. This was my platform and encouraging others is what I felt most confident about. These are the reasons why when I didn't win as I assumed I would, I felt like a piece of my soul withered up and died. I didn't really talk to anyone or express all of the emotions that I felt. However, I did begin to question my voice. I began to question if the people I thought were my friends were really my friends. I began to question if God was even there because why would He let me feel like this? What do you do when you feel so certain that where you're going is where you're supposed to be going and then all of a sudden you hit a dead-end road? I thought, *is it even possible to come up from this place? Is it even possible to move forward after this level of heartbreak? Is it even possible to dream again? How do you even know what your dream is? How does one choose a dream? How do you know if you're walking down the path that you're supposed to be walking down?*

Dream, Build, Repeat.

All of these questions and thoughts are exactly what we will explore. We are going to discover the meaning of a dream. We're going to find out how to qualify a dream. My ultimate goal is to encourage you to start believing in your dreams again, especially if you have felt like your dreams have died, or it is too late for you, or your season has passed. You are in the right place. You picked up this book for a reason. You will turn the pages and become encouraged again.

My hope is that as you read these words you don't read my story, but you see how there are elements of my journey that apply to where you are as a dreamer, a builder, and a life changer. My desire is that you take the words from the following pages and apply them, internalize them, and rediscover your dream. You ready?

two

Roots

What would you do with your life if you were not bound by the opinions of others?

This was a question that I asked myself. Why was I even concerned and consumed with what others thought of me? Where did that come from? Was this the path that I even wanted for myself?

You see, when you live your life according to the standards of other people, you begin to make decisions according to the standards of other people. Those decisions lead to action, which leads to living life according to the standards and opinions of other people. I realized that I was unable to answer the question above for myself. I had no idea why I had chosen my college major. I had no idea why I was on that current path except that I thought that it was where I was supposed to be. My thinking was based on people's expectations and what they said I'd be good at, but is that what I really wanted? Now that the rug had been ripped out from under me after the Miss Claflin pageant, I had no idea what I truly wanted to do. It was hard to distinguish facts from fiction. It was hard to distinguish what was real and what was fake, and it was hard to distinguish where my decisions ended and other people's decisions for me began.

As I was journaling and reflecting, I started to think back to the beginning. I thought back to childhood. I tried to remember what life was like before things got complicated. I started to think back to that pure, unadulterated joy from childhood. Don't get me wrong. I don't want to paint the picture that my childhood was without struggles and trials, but quite frankly, there were some great times during childhood and the more I reflected on the past, the more clarity I received for my future. You see, the past has the ability to make or break you. The past has the ability to build you up or tear you down. So I chose to look back to discover what naturally caught my attention, the activities that I thoroughly enjoyed, and even what caused me trouble during my youth.

There was this beautiful stage in Topeka, Kansas. It had lights, it had pizazz, it had the amazing features that every three-year-old needs in her life, and it was the very first stage that I stepped onto. This "stage," if you will, was located right next to the fireplace in my childhood home, and it was my domain. I hopped up on to that brick stage and sang to thousands upon thousands of adoring fans at The Apollo. I gave my fans a monologue on Broadway, and waved across that stage as Miss America. Some people viewed *my stage* as just a regular fireplace, but for me it was a place where my childhood dreams came true.

The very first play that I performed was during pre-kindergarten. I had the distinguished honor and pleasure to be a magpie in the play. A magpie, if you don't know, is a little black bird, but what I remember about that homemade costume that my neighbor Mrs. Pat Thomas made was that it was blue. (In fact, my mom told the teachers that she refused to have me, the only child of color, portrayed as a little black bird. The teachers were not pleased… but we were!) It was blue and it draped over my little arms. I had a little hat, and it was covered in gorgeous blue feathers. I wore that magpie costume out. I'm telling you, I practiced my lines every free moment with memories of being on that stage feeling alive.

As the budding actress that I was, I looked to my parents and I said, "Hey, I need to do this again. This brings me joy. This makes me happy. This is the place where I feel the most alive," (obviously, in all of the elegance of a four-year-old). My parents scoured the area and found that there was a musical called Wee Pals playing in Topeka. I auditioned, and of course I will say it, knocked it out of the park. To be honest, I just remember singing one song, and that was that. No fear, just ready to take on the world. I became the youngest cast member of Wee Pals. At the ripe old age of four, that's when purpose first winked at me. I had the honor, privilege, and joy to learn songs and to act alongside children in a groundbreaking musical.

I loved it. Our cast performed a few shows, and during one of the dress rehearsals, I remember looking up and thinking that I saw a little flash of hope, but not really understanding where it came from. A couple of days later I learned that there is a picture of me laughing and playing with dog ears. I was playing a dog, General Lee. Classy, I know. There I was at four years old stealing the show, headlining as General Lee. It's amazing how purpose meets you where you are. I loved the spotlight. It's hard to say that now because I think it sounds a little vain. However, the true reason that I loved the spotlight was because it was fun to be on stage bringing others joy. After that play, I decided that I wanted to become an actress.

Dream, Build, Repeat.

Pause and Reflect: Your dream isn't necessarily your purpose, but your dream gets you on the path to purpose. Do you remember your first childhood dream? Was it to be a famous ball player or to be the next big kid star? While you might have missed the window to actually pursue that, go deeper now. What was your motivation behind the dream? The motivation is usually more important than the dream itself and the method by which you accomplish that dream.

I continued through life and through school and I realized more and more that what I loved the most (being helpful, bringing people joy, and speaking up for important issues) were not always accepted or welcomed, because after all, who listens to a child? Who wants to take advice and be influenced by others younger than themselves, especially when that person is a child?

The next year after starring in the Wee Pals play, I continued my matriculation at a prestigious private school in Topeka, Kansas, and there I was living my best life as anyone could in kindergarten. I remember two distinct events from my two years at that school.

First, for whatever reason, our teacher stepped out of the classroom and she told us to be quiet and to be on our best behavior. I was determined to follow her instructions. However, lo and behold, I looked around and my fellow classmates were goofing off. I couldn't believe they weren't following the teacher's instructions. I knew this was unacceptable. After all, I grew up in a military household. Rules were meant to be followed. I pulled out one of those little blue plastic chairs with the three slits on the back, and I stood on the chair and I shouted to everyone, "Be quiet!" They didn't listen, and I shouted again, "Everyone be quiet!" As soon as those words left my mouth, the teacher came back in the room, snatched me off the chair, and said, "Casey, you're in time out." Of course I couldn't understand why I was in time out because I was the one who was enforcing what she had said, but it taught me that regardless of what's right, regardless of what is accepted, *my* voice should not be used in that manner. My voice was out of place. After that, any time that I would witness an injustice, I found myself questioning whether or not to say anything. Will I get in trouble? Is this my place? Is this what I should be doing? All of those questions would rush to my mind based on that one small experience from pre-kindergarten and kindergarten.

In my second silencing experience, I was sitting at a table in school and a girl was sitting across from me who had a cold. The balls of tissue were beside her and the teacher was on the other side trying to help her with an art project. Art is not my strong suit. It's not my gift or an area where I feel talented. In art, I earned an S grade for "Satisfactory" every nine weeks, except once when I got an E grade for "Excellent" in the fifth grade. Therefore, I found myself trying to figure out what on earth I was going to draw for this project. I looked down at my paper to find inspiration and *voila* it comes to me. I think about my neighbor, Mrs. Pat Thomas, and all the little cats that she had and would let me play with after school. I decided to draw the most amazing cat the world had ever seen. As I began to draw my cat and everything starts to take shape, the girl across from me, let's just call her, Erica. Erica, looks over at my paper and tells the teacher that she is going to draw a cat. I shot my head up in utter disbelief. The next logical step was to call her a copycat. I could not believe that this girl looked over at my beloved Picasso-like painting and decided that she was going to copy it.

The injustice! I mean, could she not be original? I just didn't understand. The teacher sent me to time out for calling Erica a copycat. This was very confusing because even in kindergarten I understood the definition of a copycat. Copycat means that you looked at something and you took it as your own (i.e. plagiarism) and I was being punished for someone else's lack of ingenuity. It was heartbreaking, but it also made me quite upset because I did not feel that I had done anything wrong. Again, all I wanted was for her to be original and I wanted my work to be appreciated for the masterpiece that it was. I sat in time out the rest of the day. My mom came to pick me up and the teacher told her that I had been in time out. My mom was confused because I was not one to get into too much trouble despite the previous story, and she tried to figure out what I did to earn timeout.

The teacher looked at her square in her eye and said, "Because she would not apologize," and my mom looked at me inquiring why I hadn't apologized. I responded very clearly, that I had done nothing wrong, therefore, I didn't need to apologize. That was that. I was very clear about what I wanted. Very clear that I wanted other people to thrive in what they were doing, not thrive in what I was doing. Again, I was silenced for speaking my truth and those two small incidents caused me to question the validity of my voice. With that being said, as you read (and possibly chuckle) through these stories, I want you to think back to times when you experienced a level of trauma or a level of injustice that caused you to question yourself and later show up as less than your natural self. Think about those things because if you don't deal with the roots of the negativity that you experienced, then you will continually manifest that negativity in your life.

As I thought back over those instances and laughed, I also had to reflect on the positive and the negative memories. Both greatly impact the direction of our lives. If we don't deal with them, not only will we begin to manifest the negativity over and over again, but we won't be able to move past it because we start to cast those ideas and ideals onto future circumstances and experiences. It's only natural to begin to view life through a crooked, skewed lens based on previous experiences.

Aside from being in the spotlight, loving to take action, and taking the lead, I also uncovered my love for business and entrepreneurship. While I knew that my ultimate end game was to be an actress, the way in which I got there was going to be by a "side hustle." Of course, at the time I didn't realize that I would create multiple businesses before the age of eighteen. However, I created my very first business in Clemson, South Carolina. I had visited my grandparents in rural Virginia and my grandfather used to go to this Farmer's Market at the RFK stadium in DC, and there would be so many vendors—way too many for me to count. As I was growing up, I always heard my grandfather say that he was going to the market or he went to the market or he was at the market. He was always talking about the market. He sold peanut brittle, peanuts, and sometimes my grandmother would sell things like cakes and pies and Southern sweets because she was an amazing baker.

Whenever I visited my grandparents, I would hang with my grandfather and watch him get ready for the flea market. He would prepare by frying up these peanuts in a big frying pot. Honestly, I am on the more selective side about foods that I enjoy eating. Peanuts and tree nuts were not on my list. I did not like nuts, but there was something about the ones that my grandfather would make. They were delicious, fried and salty, like everything should be! One day my grandfather asked if I wanted to make some money. Obviously, my answer was YES, because allowance did not exist at my house. He handed me several bags of peanuts and said I could sell them to the people I knew when I returned home.

So many questions come to my mind. What should I do? *What's my market? Who's my target audience?* I didn't ask any of those questions. Instead, I just agreed and knew that I would charge $2.50 per Ziploc bag. I gathered my bags of salted peanuts and made my way home.

Considering that this was my first business, I didn't understand inventory, profitability, or branding. I just knew that I had these peanuts and they were worth $2.50 each, and if I sold enough, I would have some cash. I took them to the place where I had a captive audience and could possibly sweet talk and charm potential customers.

I went to the beauty shop, after all, I would spend five to eight hours there on Saturdays. As I sat there getting my relaxed hair straightened, curled, and spritzed, as everyone did in the nineties, I would sell peanuts. Who turns down a cute little nine-year-old with a fresh 'do? Nobody. I was in business! There I was earning coins by selling peanuts, and I learned to appreciate the fact that I could make my own money. As a young salesperson, I became super comfortable with talking to different types of people in all age ranges, which later lead to me becoming one of the top Girl Scout cookie sellers. I continued to hold several entrepreneurial sales jobs. I sold everything from stadium chair backs and pizza to collegiate donation packages and education technology. No matter where I worked, people would consistently ask me how I always hit my numbers to be repeatedly recognized as a top producer. As I am writing this, I'm having flashbacks of all of those side hustles that provided me a world of entrepreneurial experiences. I didn't realize how much selling peanuts, Girl Scout cookies, and chair back covers for the middle school band would impact me at the time, but those experiences provided me with a solid foundation in business success. I learned that the key to becoming the top sales-person in each position was building relationships and getting to know people. I became really great at connecting with potential consumers and building their trust. Overtime, I began teaching and mentoring others on how to apply the same success strategies to their positions.

The confidence that I had with people came from the roots of dancing and singing on stage to selling peanuts at the hair salon. The experiences that you have as a child can make or break you, and the good news is that you have the power to choose.

Pause and Reflect: Think about what came naturally to you as a child, before everyone said what was or was not possible. What were you attracted to before you thought that it wasn't possible? Who were you before you started to mold, mend, and adjust to the expectations of others? Those roots will begin to remove the scales from the eyes of your purpose. You'll begin to see purpose and trends and notice what you loved. Through this book, you'll begin to build your life around those things that came naturally to you versus what you have conditioned yourself to love and ultimately become good at. What if, instead of just being "good," there is greatness awaiting you once you tap into what you were really created and designed to do?

Marshawn Evans Daniels, the writer of this book's foreword, always says that there are things that we are good at because we're taught to be good at them. Yet, there are things that we are amazing at that we have never done. Those newly discovered gifts are at the core of who you are. However, so many struggle to find them underneath the depths of the expectations of others. I dare you to take this time to review your past and reflect on where you've been. Think back to the good, the bad, the ugly. Consider the memories that are attractive to you and heal from the experiences that were negative. You are grounded in your roots, but don't let them keep you in a familiar place of stagnation and complacency.

three

Blending

If not addressed, rejection will dim your brilliance.

The first lesson that life taught me was to wear a mask. Life probably taught you a similar lesson. We have been trained to wear a mask in order to make others feel comfortable. We've been taught that we can't and shouldn't air our dirty laundry for other people to see. We've been taught to highlight the best, contour out the problem areas, while emphasizing the good and minimizing the shortcomings. We've been taught to wear a mask and there are some of us who have become so comfortable in our masks that we don't even realize we're wearing one. When that happens, we think that *this* is actually how we look, we think that *this* is actually our personality. We think that *this* is actually our idea when instead we have become clones of others and shells of ourselves to match what others deem acceptable. A mask. We've become so comfortable wearing a mask that when people don't wear masks, we talk about them. *Can you believe that his child did that? Can you believe that she was busted...again? Can you believe that she posted that on social media? Does he not know how to use a filter?* In this society of social media and "sharing everything great" we become so focused on painting pictures of perfection that we don't recognize authenticity when we see it. We not only fail to recognize authenticity, but we don't appreciate it either. We as a society will pick apart other people's imperfections instead of embracing them and saying "thank you for being honest and real." We don't thank authentic people for taking the time to share their struggles with us. We judge them. Maybe I just said "we" so I wouldn't feel alone in this. Maybe it's just me, but I bet if you're honest, you've done it at least once.

I love makeup, but I don't wear a fully made up face that often. I might apply a little bit of foundation, some mascara, lipstick and possibly a brow, because things must be snatched. Let me tell you that anytime I have a professional make-up artist (MUA) "beat my face" (translation: give me a great makeover), there's a difference. There's a huge difference between what I can do by myself on my best day to what a professional MUA can do in two minutes on her worst day. My typical appointment with a professional artist starts with her prepping my face. She chooses the right colors, snatches an eyebrow and proceeds to do the things that I don't know how to do. The artist adds the contour, shimmer highlight, dramatic winged liner topped with a good pair of lashes. I look amazing every time. I know it sounds cocky, but honestly when you get a good makeup artist, you should be cocky.

However, I run into this small problem. This isn't real life. At the end of the day, I have to wash it off. I wipe away the lipstick, the eyeliner, the shadow, and the artistry. The only thing remaining is my actual face. Suddenly, I don't have enough brows, and my cheekbones aren't defined enough. My eyes look bald without the eyelashes, and then I begin to notice the flaws that I didn't even realize were there until I got a glimpse of what was possible.

Blending

I equate wearing lashes, contouring, highlighting my face to this idea of putting on a mask. Don't get me wrong, I love makeup. I love how it makes me feel, but I also have to remember that my face does not look that way at all times. Wearing makeup is an enhancement, but it is not who I am. I have to realize that I must be comfortable with the way I look *with* and *without* makeup. That simple fact is one that is missing in today's society, especially with social media. Since the Internet is forever, we have to put on our best face always. We have to Facetime with a full face of makeup. We have to spell check everything and write a creative, yet effortless sounding caption. Everything must be perfect to impress these people who we don't even know in real life. Slowly but surely, blending in begins.

My first experience with blending in was back when I lived in Kansas. I was born in Indiana and I moved to Kansas when I was about two years old, and so Kansas was all that I knew. I became accustomed to being the only student in a classroom who looked like me. To add another layer of complexity, I was the only girl in my grade who looked like me. Yet, I didn't think too much about it because it was my normal. I liked most of the people who I went to school with and they liked me. My skin color was never an issue amongst my classmates. I don't remember any evidence of anything weird happening based on the color of my skin. Everything was great. I gained skills to recognize which group of people listened to pop and which group listened to gospel and R&B. Code switching starts early, y'all!

When I moved to South Carolina, halfway through second grade, I was so excited to walk into a place and not be the only brown face. I remember going home and telling my parents about the diversity in my school. It's laughable. My town was about eight percent minority, so it's not like there were that many non-Caucasians, but it was significantly more people of color than what I was used to. I was excited to find new friends at school who could relate to me in a new way.

When I started this new school I assumed that I would be instant friends with certain kids because we looked alike. Again, laughable. Apparently that was a silly idea because this was the first time that I had ever experienced discrimination from classmates based on my race or skin color. Now this time instead of discrimination coming from someone of another culture or race, I encountered people who looked like me who told me that I wasn't black enough. This is a completely different story and another topic than what we're going to address, but I remember struggling with their treatment of me and I asked them, "How can you even act like a color?"

I thought that since we had something in common, surely we should be friends, but I quickly realized that not everyone who looks like me is going to be on my team and not every person who doesn't look like me is my enemy. My dad, Carl Sharperson, Jr., writes that in his book, *Sharp Leadership*. This was an early learning experience for me and I was sad about it. It was the first time that I had ever felt rejection and to be rejected by people who looked like me was doubly hurtful. Yet I moved on and continued to live my life, but my goal for the rest of elementary school was to blend in. I just wanted to wear the things that other kids were wearing, sound the way that other kids sounded, do the things that other kids did. I just wanted to fit in.

Blending

I loved my second grade teacher in Kansas. Moving to South Carolina was not only a culture shift, but there was also an educational shift. Before moving, I hadn't really been in too much trouble in school. I definitely had never gotten in trouble in my second grade teacher's class in Kansas. South Carolina was different. My new second grade teacher had these groups of four desks all over the room. Two boys sat in the desks directly across from me, and from the very beginning, one of the boys in my cluster started to make it his habit to create commotion that would disrupt the class. The teacher would come over to investigate who did what. Like clockwork, the boy would blame everything on me. I would try to plead my case, but I was also the new kid competing with the children of high-powered executives in town. There I was getting marks on the board (these marks outed the "problem kids" in the class), which is the worst nightmare of a kid who loves to be number one in class. I don't know if you remember that system or if you had that system in your elementary school, but it was horrifying for me as an overachiever and a person who always wanted to blend in and follow the rules. Marking my name on the board was incredibly embarrassing and traumatizing. It happened consistently and it came to a point where I didn't even fight it anymore. As I sat minding my business at my desk, I did not understand why this person kept blaming things on me and why this new teacher couldn't see the real me. Of course it was all about social status. Later, I learned that this boy's mother was very high in the local government, and the teacher showed favoritism toward him. Regardless, I knew for a fact that I was not her favorite student and I did not feel like she cared about me or my experience. This fed into the rejection narrative that I was slowly building from both my peers and the authority figures in my life.

Needless to say, moving was a very hard transition for me. I cried almost every day for four months asking when we were going to go back to Kansas. I missed my old friends and my old life. I spent my ninth birthday in the hotel suite that we were living in at the time, begging my parents to take us back to my place of comfort, my home.

Finally, I came to the realization that I was never going to please that teacher or my classmates. According to the majority of my peers, I was not black enough. According to my new teacher, I could not follow instructions. I was no longer standing out in a positive way, so I began to quiet down and blend into the background. These elementary school experiences taught me that I would not be accepted as my natural self. I would always have to fight to convey the real me and the actual truth.

Pause and Reflect: What narratives have you accepted as truth in your life? What have you allowed people to say about you that did not line up with your true self?

By middle school, I'd made some peace with those who had previously called out my differences and we were cool. I realized that people were fickle and if they wanted to, they could change their minds in a moment. I became a professional floater and a support system for anyone who wanted one. I rationalized that if I was a good friend, I would attract good friends. This was sophisticated rationale for a twelve year old. I had a new goal, which the overachiever in me loved. My goal was to be a really great friend by planning all of the events and outings, decorating people's lockers for birthdays, and all sorts of fun things. I became the ultimate social butterfly. In fact, I would switch tables every single lunch period to make sure that none of my "friends" felt left out. I would sit with a certain group of people one time and another group of people another time. As far as I could tell, everyone liked me, didn't want to fight me, and we were getting along fine. I fought hard to maintain this balance of being the perfect friend. This required me to be everything to everyone. Additionally, I played clarinet in the band, cheered, ran track, ran cross country, participated in Girl Scouts, and took tumbling classes. I was involved in just about everything. I had found acceptance in achievement. I was blending. I slowly realized that I was being accepted for the skills, talents, and effort I brought to the party. My ever-growing group of friends enjoyed my presence, and that acceptance gave me so much life. I thrived as the go-to person who people called when they were struggling. I owned the title of "strong friend" and wore it with immense pride. However, the problem with being friends with everyone is that you're not truly friends with anyone. I had mastered the superficial relationships that had just enough depth for me to know people's entire lives, while simultaneously not sharing mine. I had all the friends and none of the friends. The rejection narrative continued to build.

Pause and Reflect: As a strong friend you learn to place other's problems above your own. You get comfortable as a support system who doesn't have support. You adjust the weight of the world on your shoulders until you crack under the pressure. If you have the privilege not to wear this title, identify if whether or not you have a "strong friend." This is the ultimate, unbalanced dysfunction that is learned during childhood friendships, familial relationships, and life circumstances. Let me be the one to let you know that you need relationships that pour into you, not just relationships that drain you.

While I was decorating other people's lockers and supporting them during good and bad times, that same courtesy was not extended back to me. I didn't have much to show for my friendships except some instant messaging contacts and a large group of surface relationships. Slowly, I made less and less of myself available. I learned to become a master at being very likable without being offensive. I learned the art of people-pleasing without major moral compromise. It's a skill, believe me.

Fast forward to college when I became the ultimate master of blending. Honing in on the major lessons from kindergarten through twelfth grade, I was ready to take on my final lesson in pre-adulting. I had finally understood that not everyone was going to agree with me or share my thought processes, but we could still get along because I would put on my mask to audibly agree and silently disagree. I would not make waves, I'd coast, because that's what I was used to. I continued on the path of being heavily involved in anything that interested me. As a result, I was booked and busy. I joined several organizations including Student Government, the cheerleading squad, Alpha Kappa Alpha Sorority, and others. Due to my commitments, I had no free time. I was scheduling time to eat, sleep, do homework, and spend time with my friends.

When you have limited free time, you have limited time alone to reflect and to think about life. I never took the time to ask myself if I actually enjoyed all of the things I was committed to. I had no idea what I liked or disliked. I was in grind mode as a coping mechanism to avoid the rejection of my past. There was a part of me that knew if I separated myself from the titles and business that I would see the truth of my life. Honestly, I wasn't ready to face it. I didn't want to face the fact that many of the people I surrounded myself with might not be my friends. I was starting to realize that I had a lot of associates and no deep connections with people. However, instead of dealing with truth, I kept filling the space and hoping that these people and these achievements and these opportunities would fill the relational void that I felt in my heart.

Instead, some of those commitments ended up silencing me. I found myself spending time with people who didn't appreciate my gifts or understand me. I began to quiet what came naturally to me and adjust to what people wanted and expected. This was especially prevalent in my high school and college cheerleading squads. In both instances, I started out as an inexperienced freshman, who the upperclassmen were dead set on "breaking." I noticed myself constantly proving that I earned my spot to be there. I worked three times harder, did not complain, and I allowed my skills to speak for themselves. Still, I would make suggestions about what to wear, what to do, how we could make an impact, and was shut down. In fact, in college, I was told that my ideas were stupid and why would anyone think that my suggestions were good ideas. All of that negativity began to seep into my soul. I believed that I didn't have expertise to add, despite the proof in the form of medals, trophies, statistics, and skills. I began to believe that I was only good at performance, not creative solutions. Eventually, I earned some street credibility, but the damage was already done.

Pause and Reflect: You see, even though I tried to dial it back, there was still a bit of my purpose starting to shine through. As much as I wanted to blend in, there were elements of my nature that couldn't be stifled. Can you identify an area in your life that you have tried to silence or shut down that you simply couldn't? Many times the reason that you've been shut down or dismissed by others isn't because you didn't have anything to add, but because your brilliance was too complex for some people to understand.

As a result, I self-corrected, self-regulated, and self-edited as a means to preserve my ego. I accepted what people said as truth, rather than opinion. I thought that I lacked creativity and that my problem solving skills were subpar, although these qualities were clearly evident in my life and came naturally to me. This is how doubt forms. You look at what you think should occur to what actually happened; you measure, assess, and question your worth and abilities.

Doubt manifested regarding my ability to speak with fluidity and confidence, if you've met me, you know speaking is my God-given gift. I started viewing my personality as "too much." I learned to second guess myself instead of fearlessly charging ahead with an idea. I learned to analyze and analyze and analyze to make sure that everything was perfect before I took action.

Blending. Mask-wearing. Perfecting. Protecting. Analyzing.
These are all things that we use to cope with people not recognizing the amazing people that we are. Let me rephrase that: you are amazing. You have gifts and talents. Your voice needs to be heard. Your ideas are exceptional.

Blending

The world needs to know who you are authentically, without the mask. You don't have to accept what has been said about you or to you. You don't have to suppress who you are at your core. Your accent is exactly what it should be. You skin color is the perfect shade. Your hair texture is beautiful. Your height is ideal.

Don't allow negativity from people to stunt who you were meant to be. Those negative seeds begin to chip away at self-confidence. They begin to point you in the direction that other people want you to go rather than the direction that you are designed to go. Blending molds you into a clone of everyone else. It suppresses what makes you unique and causes you to despise the things that make you special. Blending in is what's keeping you from accomplishing your dreams. Are you ready to do the work to stop blending and start shining?

Dream, Build, Repeat.

PART II

BUILD

Dream, Build, Repeat.

four
Step 1: Realize

The disappointments of life can be used to hold you back or propel you forward in the direction of purpose.

Who are you? When you leave the eyes of other people, who are you? When you get home from work, close the door, and collapse on the couch, what do you think about? Where is your life going? Those are the types of questions that I had to ask myself to dive deep into this journey of self-discovery. As a person who prided herself on "having it all together" all the time and being a problem fixer, I found myself in a situation that I could not solve. *How good of a "fixer" am I, if I can't even fix myself and if I don't know who I am?* I thought. I had spent so much time molding, forming, and shaping to people's expectations of me that I truly, honestly did not know the real me. I didn't know what I enjoyed or what I couldn't stand. I felt like a shell of a person.

When I saw everything that I expected crashing down, I had to sit down and figure out my identity at the root rather than this surface level viewpoint that I was so used to portraying and other people were so used to seeing. I had an awakening. There was a moment when I sat on my bed looking at that white brick wall won-

49

dering where to go next. Have you found yourself in a position where everything around you is unfamiliar? When you begin to question the authenticity of the people you've trusted? When you question who's really in your corner and who's really just pretending?

I finally realized this farce wasn't working for me. This image of perfection that I had sold was a lie. Whether ill intended or not, it was still a lie. It was a lie to pretend that everything was okay when just a few months prior my father had been diagnosed with cancer and just a few months before that there was strife between my parents and I. As much as I wanted to pretend, the truth was forcing its way out.

If you haven't already experienced this, *your* awakening moment is bound to come. You must identify the issue and realize there is another way. That way is a journey that's sometimes unpleasant, but always rewarding.

I chose to spend time getting to know me. I spent time apart from people to just dig into the depths of me for truth and discovery. Prior to that, I found myself staying busy, surrounded by people and dodging time alone. Why? Because when we're exhausted, our brains don't wander to the voids of relationship status, friendships, work, school, family or anything else we might be dodging. Not everyone self-medicates with too many pills or too many drinks. Some of us self-medicate with too many commitments and countless accolades, looking for praise for a quick confidence high.

When you don't enjoy spending time with yourself, it's a sign. For me, it wasn't that I didn't enjoy who I thought I was. My issue was when I was by myself, I truly felt alone and disconnected.

Staying busy was my best "drug." It allowed me to avoid my disappointments and mask the fact that I truly didn't feel connected with some of the people in my life.

In the past, I learned that quality time was my top love language. However, even too much of a good thing can be destructive. I was spending time with people to fill voids, but even that failed because I had built surface-level relationships. None of those people could tell you anything deep or significant about my life. They didn't know me, and I didn't know them.

I substituted those true deep friendships and relationships with activities and accolades. I joined every organization and was an active part of everything. I tried new things, which is great; however, when you put that on top of insecurities and false expectations, it's a recipe for dysfunction.

Accomplishments, recognition, and pats on the back were how I got high. I was compensating for the rejection I felt as a girl. Perhaps I thought that I would finally be seen and recognized for the true me. Yet, when you find validation and worth in other people's praises, it becomes a breeding ground for discontentment. What happens when the praises stop? What happens if for some reason those people no longer praise you, but they tear you down? [Insert crazy Internet trends here.]

Pause and Reflect: What's your "drug" of choice? What have you found yourself consumed by instead of dealing with difficult realities? Whether it's binging on television, food, relationships, or shopping, those distractions are not only coping mechanisms, but they are preventing the growth needed to elevate rather than stagnate.

Do you know how quickly someone can get famous online with a viral video or post? Instantly, everyone starts sliding in their DMs (inbox) boosting them up. Yet, time goes on and another story or person is trending and the first Internet star is no longer relevant. Or worse, the Internet has turned on them and suddenly, those amazing accolades and praises have turned into mean and hateful comments. This is an emotional roller coaster that you don't have to ride. You have the power to exit stage left, but the only way that you will have the power to do that is if you realize where you are. Identify how you ended up in this place of seeking validation from things and people who don't have the right and the ability to accept you, to build you up, and to even speak life into you.

———

I also realized that I thought education would gain me acceptance and validation. I thought that if I had the right letters behind my name, if I took the right classes, if I secured the right internships, then people would accept the brilliance that was within me.

I relied on those titles instead of realizing that the brilliance was innately inside of me. Education could only enhance the person I was at my core. Education and titles don't determine your worth, just as they don't determine mine. You are the secret sauce. It took a while for me to realize this, and I wanted people to tell me that I was good enough. However, it's much more powerful to know without a shadow of a doubt, "I'm dope. Period." You must know that too, and you don't have to apologize for this either. This confidence comes from your awakening moment.

Following college, I was planning to get my MBA in international business because I loved culture, building relationships, travel, and business. It seemed like the perfect way to do all the things I enjoyed. I thought that this degree was the only way to accomplish those things. I quickly saw that my awakening journey hadn't concluded when I walked across the stage at Claflin. It followed me when, yet, another door slammed in my face.

After preparing, studying, working, and striving for the GRE and GMAT entrance exams, I submitted my applications and waited. I waited for that life-changing moment when I would receive the acceptance letter to my dreams. I wanted to be accepted into the program that would teach me everything I needed to know about business, entrepreneurship, and culture. I waited for schools to tell me how much money I was worth in the form of scholarships. I waited for another entity to validate all my hard work. I knew this was the path I was supposed to take. I had no doubt in my mind. After all, just a year prior I had learned my lesson. I had my awakening moment.

The moment I received my scores, I called Jeff, the admissions counselor at my top school. I excitedly told him my number. Then it happened. He politely shared that there was a sliding scale admission, and while my score was good, and people had been accepted into the program with it, this year, I would not be admitted. In fact, he told me I was one point away.

Shocked. I'm sure he said some other fluffy stuff to try to make me feel better, but it sounded like a muffled mess. *Click* I hung up the phone. Numb. I was crushed, coming off the heels of this major disappointment with Miss Claflin to now being one point away from what was supposed to be my new dream. It was sobering to say the least.

That began my second awakening moment. No more was I going to chase people's acceptance. I wasn't chasing acceptance to school, organizations, or anything else. I refused to chase. It was too painful and too difficult. I didn't have the capacity and the space to put my eggs into these baskets that I ultimately had no control over.

Realization is sometimes difficult and always the necessary first step to build, grow, and develop a vision and dream. To realize where you are currently by embarking on a journey of self-discovery is the key to a solid foundation that cannot be shaken by the opinions and preferences of others.

To experience your own awakening, I suggest traveling to new or familiar places, both physically and within your soul/imagination. You might want to take up a new hobby or task, do something that is calming for you, participate in an activity that is clarifying for you. You might take a week away and detox from the Internet, from people, or from food. You might read this book in a local coffee shop with your favorite drink. Your journey of self-discovery might include counseling or therapy to talk through some of those issues and some of the mental blocks. I have found such value in talking out loud about my disappointments and about my fears. It's not only cathartic, but when you say things out loud, it begins to take away the power, the pain, and maybe the hurt. Things seem so challenging and so difficult and so daunting and overwhelming when you're looking at them from your internal perspective (experiencing them in your head). You may rationalize your way out of something great or stay in a toxic environment out of comfort. Yet, when you speak your truth out loud, it takes away all power. You have a choice whether to own what you hear and feel as your truth or dispel it as a lie.

Pause and Reflect: While I breezed through the retelling of being denied from every school I applied to for my MBA, know that the second awakening took time. I took months to reprogram my mindset from that of a victim to a victor. Have you allowed yourself time and space to heal from things that hurt you? No situation is too small or too big. Don't discount or discredit how you feel. Your emotions are valid, just don't allow them to keep you stuck in a victimized place.

I learned so much about myself when I started lifting weights over the past few years. It was different for me because as an athlete, I was only used to pushups, sit-ups, and activities without a lot of resistance. Yet weight training was a fantastic way for me to not only push my body to another dimension, but it also opened my eyes and showed me that I can do something that's totally out of my comfort zone and thrive. Whatever your path looks like, you should commit to developing your mind, body, and spirit.

When you commit to fine tuning the depths of your soul that have been hidden you will experience peace. Peace only comes when you realize where you are. Don't run from the journey or the discomfort. For muscles to grow, they must be broken down and rebuilt. Repeatedly. Each disappointment, each closed door, each heartbreak is an opportunity for growth and building. Without your commitment to the process, you won't be able to step into your full purpose, calling, or business destination. You must know your starting point.

Dream, Build, Repeat.

five

Step 2: Renew

***A whole, healthy dreamer is committed to self-assessment in
pursuit of growth and maturation.***

Time spent assessing how you view yourself and others is the key
to renewing your mind, body, and spirit in preparation of realizing
your dream. Without renewing the old mindset, it's impossible to
create a new reality with a fresh perspective.

Health

I realized that I had to deal with my past to figure out what con-
tributed to my current circumstance in order to move forward.
You'll never be able to live a new dream while holding on to the
toxicity of the broken things of the past. To move forward, it's im-
perative to identify unhealthy habits, unhealthy desires, and anything that is hindering you from your positive, successful future.
It's impossible to dream big if you're lacking a solid, confident
view of who you are.

Contrary to popular belief, your health is a huge factor in
accomplishing your dreams. When you eat crappy food, you feel
crappy, therefore you lack productivity. Something as small as

drinking water and eating healthy drastically improves your energy levels, mood, and productivity. When you view yourself as a whole, healthy person, then your soul will actually begin to reflect that as well.

I love to search Google and YouTube for healthy recipes, habits, and swaps. Small tweaks such as adding chia seeds and hemp seeds to yogurt, oatmeal, or a fresh smoothie is how I function during the day. I love drinking kombucha and taking vitamins to keep my immunity elevated so I have the energy to do the things that I desire to do.

Friendships

Assess friendships and how they affect you. When I evaluated my friends (or the people I called my friends), I realized that not only were they not supportive, but I was also in constant competition with them. Let's be clear. You can never, ever have a healthy relationship that is based upon or fueled by jealousy, competition, or lack of support.

If spending time with certain people causes you to doubt your worth, question your significance, or become green with envy, it's time to reassess. If you feel the need to exaggerate your successes or spend money you don't have in order to keep up with so-called friends, it's time to reassess.

Your friends can be an asset or a liability. In the same way that you should assess the friends you have, you must also assess the type of friend you have been. Why do you get upset when your friends don't support your projects? Do you support theirs? They don't call you enough? Do you check on them, just because? They don't invite you places? Do you invite them? Honestly, it's trifling to expect something out of people when you're unwilling to give the same. Friends are not mind-readers, some are close, but don't hold them to this unattainable standard of perfection. This idea was the most difficult for me to own. For years, my feelings would be hurt because I felt like I was doing things for people and giving, and they just took without reciprocating. They were living their lives, while I was silently upset and frustrated. Don't be that person. If they're takers, let them take advantage of other people. If you're silently wallowing because they can't meet your mental expectations, talk it out, figure it out, and move on.

The falsehood of being the "strong friend" needs to die. It's not possible and it robs people of the ability to be a good friend to you. Jim Rhone says that you are the average of the five people you spend the most time with. Your network, your future, your aspirations will be greatly, positively impacted or greatly negatively impacted by the people who you choose to commune with. However, this doesn't mean that you should never spend time with people who you don't deem to be "on your level." A powerful rule to live by is to be sure to have three types of people in your life. One, a person you're learning from (a mentor). Two, a person with whom you're walking a similar journey (a peer). Three, a person you're teaching and building up (a mentee). That's balance.

Relationships

The person you choose to date or marry has the potential to sky-rocket your dreams or drag them down. At the time that I was going through my renewal phase, I had just gotten out of a very toxic relationship. The relationship was not only exhausting, but it caused me to question the expectations that I had of a relationship. Were the standards too high? Were they too low? Was I unreasonable to expect certain things? Since I'm not a fan of gray areas, I decided that I needed to take a break from dating to answer those questions and figure out how not to date crazy again. A great sign of wisdom is being intentional to not repeat habits that aren't conducive to your future.

During this man-cation (yes, it's a thing), I dedicated myself to learning from people who appeared to have healthy relationships. I spent time with people who had marriages like I wanted. I read books and listened to teaching. There's so much information available and so many people ready to teach that I thought it incredibly unwise to continue to figure it out by myself. That's my mantra for EVERY area of life.

In my time off I realized what a colossal waste of time "chillin'" and "talking" was. The time and energy I spent picking out what we wanted to share on the two-for-two menu with someone I was barely interested in took time away from my passion, purpose, and dream. Understand that every time you say "yes" to something, you're saying "no" to something else. While it may be cute to get a free meal, it's untrue to say that there's not enough time to pursue your God-sized dream. There's time. You just chose to kick it instead.

Don't get me wrong, relationships are beautiful, but if you're in it just because it's comfortable or just because you don't want to be lonely, it's a cop out. Is that person pushing you to where you need to be or are they taking away precious time from those people who you are called to serve?

Purpose is attractive. When you're purpose driven, you should attract the same. Relationships should be a positive reflection and an elevation rather than a demotion of any area of your life.

Spiritual

Spirituality was the biggest driver throughout the renewal process. It's the foundation which my life is built upon. I firmly believe that you have to be grounded in belief to have any sense of peace. Immediately after I lost the Miss Claflin competition, I received a call from Mrs. Tisdale, the director of the honors program, who I affectionately call, Mama T (I dedicated this book to her). Hers was one of the only calls I answered as I was slipping into this super depressed space. Mama T was so kind to check in and of course, I acted as if I was totally fine. Then she asked me a question that changed the entire trajectory of my life.

"Casey, what are you going to do next year?" It was April of my junior year and the obvious answer was that I would return to campus next year... shame-faced. She lovingly pushed back and said, "No, you need to go somewhere. You can go to Boston, New York, or abroad. Let me know what you pick, and I'll make sure it happens."
blank stare

All the deadlines had passed. I had no idea how I was going to pay for any of it, and I had nothing but questions. Yet, when her suggestion/order came, I knew I was supposed to go abroad. It was a goal I'd had since high school, but thought it would never happen.

I purchased a passport by faith the summer before to have just in case someone called me for an all-expense-paid trip. Lesson: prepare for what you pray for.

I chose to travel to Costa Rica, which helped to rekindle my relationship with God which was on life-support at the time.

A few short months later, I was off to the most beautiful, serene countries of Costa Rica, Nicaragua, and Panama, where I could pull away and find my center. Sometimes you're so close to situations that they feel all consuming. Sometimes after heartbreak it feels like you'll never heal or get past it. Getting away to another country, the spa, the closet, or a bathroom stall is needed. It grounds you.

When I returned to the states, four months later, I had a fresh perspective. I no longer saw the loss as a detriment, but I saw it as a gift and an opportunity. I knew that everything was how it was supposed to be, which was incredibly comforting. After six months, being back on campus was a major transition. I recall getting ready for my first event and having an undeniable experience with God.

Being a part of a Greek organization (especially a Black Greek Letter Organization) comes with expectations. When you pledge you must know all of the core information about the organization. If you don't, you are most definitely going to be judged and called a poser or just a letter wearer. It's a culture. Just imagine if someone says they are a LeBron fan, but has no idea of his number, any of his stats, or the team he plays for. Being a "fan" of his is impossible. The truth is that this person probably heard someone talk about LeBron and thought he sounded cool. The same thought process goes for sororities or fraternities.

As I was getting dressed, putting on my sorority pin, I realized that I should quickly review my sorority information because I hadn't thought about it in such a long time. I had been living my best life on a beach and in a bikini and my mindset was not on my world at home

Immediately, an alarming thought followed. "You've been in the sorority for a year and a half, and you know the hundred plus year history, dates, names, everything. You have claimed to be a Christian since you were seven-years-old. How many scriptures can you quote? How would people know that you follow Christ by looking at your life?"

I stood there frozen because I knew it was the voice of God and there was no denying it. I also had no response. That was the turning point for me to realize that I hadn't really heard from God in that way before because I didn't make space for him. I also felt like the ultimate poser for my faith. I had to make a change and figure out what faith really meant to me as an adult. Your belief system and faith have to be chosen by you. It can't be passed down and caught by proximity, and I had to make a choice.

I know everybody who reads this might not be a Christian, but this can be applied to so many areas of our lives where we claim something or we absorb something just because our family did it or because people around us are doing it. If you haven't made a decision to follow what you claim to believe, and in my situation, follow God, then you're just a poser. In every area of my life I have started to ask myself, what's the fruit or result of this? How do I see the manifestation of what I'm talking about? I started studying the Bible intensely and intentionally with notes and highlighters. I ended up finding myself within the pages of the book that changed my life.

However, you define your spirituality, it should be the core of your belief system. It should encourage you and build you up. It should challenge you and make you better.

Family

Finally, it was time for family. They're the ones you don't get to choose, but you can decide how you experience them. You have an opportunity to be a witness, a light, and a positive influence on your family members. As I was assessing and letting go of a lot of negative relationships, I began to lean more on my family and start to build positive relationships. I transitioned to look at my family as friends and as a support system rather than just people who were there to give me rules, regulations, and reprimands.

If you're called to encourage, build, and help people, then not having healthy relationships and boundaries with your family members will factor into your purpose. Despite what you might think, it does affect you. So if you have relationships with your family (or those close like family), then take some time to build them. If you have strained relationships, build on those as well to get to a place of acceptable and healthy boundaries. Be the person to others that you want to have in your life, even if they don't reciprocate. If not for them, this process is for you.

At this point, I began to believe the best of others and forgive quickly. My family relationships were a start to this practice. They were a training ground to prepare me for all other relationships. We can assume that people mean us harm, but quite frankly, they might just be ignorant to their actions and our feelings. I wonder how many full-blown arguments there have been because people did not meet unstated, but assumed expectations. Maybe it's just me that feels like the whole world should just know better. Ha! In the end, believing the best and forgiving quickly as a result of my renewal process has become a way of life for me. In fact, for my immediate family, I became the "anger translator." I don't know if you have seen that comedy sketch, but my modified example is this: There are two people having a discussion. The two people are talking in circles and nothing is getting accomplished. I listen, rephrase, restate, ask for clarity, and do it again. It's hilarious, lightens the mood, and usually gets the job done. The real secret is to listen to the heart behind statements and remove the emotion..

Giving people grace in areas where it's easy to get mad instead is key in renewing your family relationships. Honestly, I am so grateful that I was mature enough to grow those familial relationships because I love them and we have so much fun together. I wouldn't trade them for anything.

My first "viral video" with family members is really funny. My brother, mom, dad, and I are all dancing... or trying to dance on the beach. It's beautiful to have those moments captured. I wonder how many moments I might not have experienced if I would have continued to hold on to past hurts and grudges. I chose to heal instead. You also have the opportunity to create new and better memories with your family, even if no one ever apologizes.

Self-talk

This last assessment step is critical. When you renew your view of who you are, then you must also look at what you say to yourself. What do you believe about yourself? What do you say when things go wrong? Do you start to beat yourself up and say, "Oh, you're so stupid! I can't believe you did that!" or "Ahh, better luck next time!" The things that you say about yourself and to yourself reveal the truth (about your self-esteem). Most would be horrified if the thoughts they had about themselves were on display for others to read.

I'll be honest, if I talked about others or to others how I spoke to myself, my life would look like a reality show with tables flipped and hair flying. It was (and still can be) a huge problem. The impossible standard that I was holding myself to was unattainable. So, if you're like me, run your thoughts through this filter: "Would I say this to someone I loved? Would I say this about my best friend? Would I mind if this thought was displayed on a random jumbotron somewhere?" If the thought doesn't pass that foolproof test, then you shouldn't say it to yourself or about yourself.

With this renewal phase, I began to declare the things that I believed (or wanted to believe) about myself. I was honest and recognized that I was not the most patient person yet, but one day I would be. I would still declare that "I am patient. I am kind. I am giving, I am gifted." Speaking declarations and affirmations will really change how you see yourself and also how you interact with others. Create a list of goals and make vision board. This will also help you visualize and become the person who you want and strive to be. Keep them in front of you to stay focused and refrained from cursing yourself out or calling you out of your own name. Those are positive infusions that will renew how you see yourself, and as you renew how you see yourself, other people will begin to see you that way as well. Try writing out ten "I am" statements that you want to see manifest in your life and say them daily for a week. See how your mind shifts!

Dream, Build, Repeat.

six

Step 3: Review

Moving forward requires walking backwards.

Yes, it's an oxymoron and yes, it's true. Review your life and where you've been, what you've gone through, and what you've experienced. This will give you insight into where you should go, your areas of influence, what you have overcome, and where you have experienced victory which allowed you to gain expertise. Even through your crying, laughing, growth, stagnation, blending, suppressing, there were still moments of purpose that you'll find. Start shining through the hard times and radiating through the good times. Avoiding your past is like getting a manual to a complex system, refusing to read it, but continuously getting to one point only to start building over again. It's not productive because when you refuse to look at the past, your life will begin to look like a negative cycle where you repeat the same experiences and mistakes over again. Your life, your business, your purpose will start to look the exact same. The circumstances might change, but the outcome will be the same. You might find that you are a builder, that you love to come up with new ideas, and that you build and build. You build until you get to a point where something happens when it all crumbles, you get bored, you get tired, you get frustrated, and you quit...but guess what?

You're a builder, and so you go and you build a new building again. You build, and all of a sudden, it gets hard. All of a sudden, you get frustrated. All of a sudden, you don't get the funding that you want and you decide that it isn't for you. That is a cycle that will keep you from your purpose and destiny. However, you will not realize those patterns until you take the time to review and walk back over the good, the bad, the ugly, the happy, and the sad moments in your life. No matter what happened in your past, it made you who you are — every single moment and experience laid the foundation for the excellence that is within you, so don't despise your story. Don't despise the experiences that you've had because they made you. I remember that moment when I realized I had to go back into my past, and I had a mini freak out moment. You know that moment where you say, "Oh, I've been avoiding the truth for so long that I don't think I even know what the truth is," right? Your past can look so scary. It can be so unnerving. It can be so hurtful that you sacrifice your future trying to neglect your past, but now it's time to review, and the great thing about this is that if you don't know your purpose or if you're unclear of your purpose, this review phase will begin to open up your eyes in a new way. If you do, in fact, know your purpose, reviewing your past will begin to illuminate experiences that you didn't even realize were building blocks for you. It will begin to illuminate new ideas or maybe even encourage and strengthen your resolve that you are truly an expert in a certain area because you've gone through the fire. Don't neglect this step. This step is arguably the most important step of this process. You have to look back in order to move forward.

In kindergarten, I was in love with all things fun. I loved to be in the spotlight as I mentioned before, but I also really loved to help people, and this is something that I noticed as I reviewed my life to figure out my purpose. I could see that I was doing what I do now even in kindergarten. In kindergarten, I came up with games and strategies. In kindergarten, I selected my clothes and dressed other people. In kindergarten, I led groups of people, but also in kindergarten, when my school received superlatives at the end of the school year, *I just knew* my teacher would have rave reviews about me. She gave the "Most Helpful" distinction to the girl with pigtails. She gave "Best Leader" to the guy with the bowl cut fade, and the girl with the gorgeous curls and big blue eyes and glasses received "Most Creative." So when it came to my turn, I was excited. I knew that I was a leader. I knew that I was creative. I knew that I loved to entertain people, so my name was called, and I strolled up to get my award. My superlative was "Miss Busy Body." I know, I know. You can chuckle, and I even laugh at it now, but my teacher did not mean it as a compliment. We know that she tried to dress it up as a compliment, but it was most definitely a way to say that I was in people's business and I needed to mind my own. Now that I've grown up and matured a bit, I can consider some other words and adjectives to describe the experience between me and that teacher. She could have called me "Most Inquisitive" because I wanted to clarify the instructions. I wanted to learn the needs of my peers and how I could help. Now that I have a business mindset, I would call that younger me a future consultant because she knew how to ask the right questions to get the right answers in order to get results, but my teacher didn't see that. She saw me as being a busy-body. There I was excited for a superlative only to be knocked down to realize that it wasn't in fact positive. I include this story to remind you that people will see the gift inside of you and will often distort, twist, and manipulate it to look negative when in fact it is a positive. In fact, that gift could be your bread and butter. Don't discount any of your experiences: that trait that once got you in trouble, that mouth that used to get popped because you talked too much, all those moments you spent daydreaming at amazing buildings and architecture may have gotten you in trouble as a kid, but they have the potential to pay your bills (and more than that), to change lives and to impact generations, now.

You might have been cut down and criticized for that thing in the past, but don't allow those past superlatives to become your truth. Your past is not your truth. You have the choice to decide whether you will accept the labels that have been placed on you or if you will reject them.

Since I loved the spotlight, as I mentioned before, my family put me in dance. I was that girl who had the little beads in her hair with braids, bows, and burettes. I wore frilly tutus with glitter and sequence, tap shoes, and shiny gold stockings that every little girl wears on stage. The dance studio I attended was a dream. Upon entering, I was greeted by frills and feathers and awesome combinations of clothing. This is probably where I acquired my over-the-top fashion sense.

I can recall focusing extremely hard on performing the right dance moves with hands on hips, smiles on lips, and all of the other details we were taught. I loved that studio so much, but at the end of my second grade year, my parents told me that we were moving, and I would not be able to attend any longer. I had my final recital and I still remember it clearly. We danced to "God Bless America" as our finale scene. I still remember a little bit of the choreography as well, but what sticks out so clearly in my mind is what my dance instructor said to my parents and I as we were leaving. "Casey has front row potential," she told us. She meant well, but what she was saying is that one day I could work my way up to the front, but in that moment, I was only good enough to be in the back. I was in the back. I was on the side. I was in a corner, because she didn't think I was ready to be in the front. The lesson here is that people will see the potential in you, but they won't necessarily provide you the opportunity to step into that potential. There are people who see your potential. They know you have what it takes, but they refuse to give you an opportunity. For you, it may mean that instead of receiving that promotion, your boss says, "Oh, we love you, but you're not there yet. We know that you can do the job, but someone else is going to do it just a smidge better." Someone else has two days more experience than you, so they see you as just "potential." They know that you can do the job, but they're unwilling to allow you the space to prove it. So what do you do? What do you do when you find yourself with the choice between going in the direction of your potential or staying in the exact same place? You must make your own opportunity. You must become so good that they cannot deny you from your front row space. I could have said, "Okay, I have front-row potential. That means I'll never be on the front row, so I should quit or stay in the background." However, that's not what I chose to do. I decided to become the best version of me.

Over time, I became more and more confident in my potential so that when people experienced me, they began to ask the question, "Why is she in the back? Why is she there?" That's the power of being the best that you can possibly be and doing your very best work regardless of your position. Eventually, people will begin lobbying for you and fighting on your behalf. You don't always have to do all the footwork. There will be a point where you are steady working, working, working, producing, producing, producing, and people in the background who you don't even know are watching will see your fruitfulness. When they see your faithfulness, they will begin to speak on your behalf in order to elevate you. As they are elevating you in the background (where you have no idea), you will also begin to create your own space.

Today, you can create your own opportunity using technology. There are people who go on audition after audition, without making anything happen, but with one viral video, companies start calling them. Why? They made their own space and created their own opportunity.

You have the chance to do the same thing with your business, your future, and your dreams. You can create a space that you want to see. You can become your own public relations representative. You can become your own social media manager, and you can create a space where your work, excellence, achievements, and skills are being highlighted. On the Internet and in person, you must look at your past and not allow past experiences to prevent you from creating your own space. Too often, people get stuck in their potential and refuse to move into their promise.

When I moved to South Carolina, I met one of best friends, and we clicked instantly. We connected and decided that we were going to start a summer teaching school for children. Considering that we were both eight-years-old at the time, the only children that we had access to were her little brother and sister, and they were babies. Their ages didn't stop us. We went to the dollar store to pick up materials. We wrote the lesson plans, and began to teach them. I created the curriculum, and told my friend, "This is how we're going to do it." Today, when I look back on that time, I realize that I strategized. I planned. I taught. I executed all of those skills at age eight. Nobody knew about this other than maybe our parents and obviously her siblings, but this is something that we said we would do continuously. After the summer, we went on a hiatus that never ended, because kids have short attention spans. But that's okay, because the concept is important. Even as a child, I recognized my love for educating others who were walking where I had been and it had nothing to do with my own smarts. I just wanted to teach someone something that would make their lives easier. Although I was only eight-years-old, this is the same concept that I bring into my coaching and consulting practice for businesses and organizations. I look at where they are and I teach them how to identify the needs of their audiences, which, as you can see, often lie in one's own experiences. As a strategist, I focus on shortening people's learning curves and providing the quickest path to success based on proven systems and strategies. That's all that we were doing as children by creating this teaching curriculum. We were only in second grade and we were shortening the learning curve of children just a little younger. If you are a coach, mentor, or teacher all you are doing is teaching the person who's just a little bit behind you. You are showing someone the path that you took and simplifying the things that frustrate you and pointing them in the direction of transformation. I did that even at eight-years-old, but I would not have realized coaching, teaching, and mentoring was an innate part of me if I hadn't reviewed the past and realized that I had been doing that for over twenty years. For twenty-plus years, I had been teaching people what I already knew, helping them along their journeys and loving every single minute of it. What comes to you innately? What did people say to and about you? Perhaps they told you that you're moving too fast, doing too much, or that you're not qualified. Maybe they even deterred you in an area, such was the case with me. It doesn't mean that what they said was true, it just means that they said it. So revisit your steps since childhood and look for a clarifying moment that changed your behavior. You may not have realized that something was a trend in your life, so you can't be afraid to review your life if you want to discover the hidden threads.

My last example will come as a surprise because most people see me as kind and gentle and they don't think I ever have an unkind word to say about anyone. If that's what you think, this story is about to rock your world.

Right before my tenth grade year, my parents forced me (and I say forced because I did not want to go to this place), but they forced me to go to a science and technology summer program. We studied math, engineering and coding, nothing that remotely interested me. I didn't even like math, so this was definitely not my scene. I would not have chosen this camp for myself, but my parents had heard such great things about this program. It was a four-week program at a university in Tennessee. I didn't really love the program, but it was my first time on a college campus and so for that reason, it had an element of "cool."

When you're in high school, it's exciting to be around the college students, to see what happens on campus, go into the Caf, and eat the cafeteria food, which of course wasn't good, but it was just a foreshadowing of what was to come. During this camp filled with teenagers, there were a lot of politics involved and of course there was one crew of popular girls, who were popular in a negative sense, but people followed them because they were scared not to follow them. These girls were bullies.

Most of the other campers were scared of them, and they had a bone to pick with me. They had alluded to the fact that they thought that I thought that I was better than them. Are you keeping up with the teen drama? Coming across as stuck up was never my intention, but for a vision, this was during the time of trends such as polos from Aeropostale and Polo Ralph Lauren… with a popped collar.

There came a point towards the end of the program when I had this strong feeling that I really should go confront them about how they were treating people. As I was wrapping up my shoulder-length, chemically-relaxed hair, I knew that enough was enough and they needed to be nicer and stop causing strife. You see, I've always had an "I need to protect the underdog" mentality. I wanted to be an attorney for the majority of my life. It came from wanting to speak up for people who couldn't speak for themselves. This was one of those times. These girls were making everyone uncomfortable and no one wanted to be around them. It was difficult for us to enjoy ourselves and focus on our work because they were constantly ridiculing and insulting people.

Finally, I decided it was the time to make a change, so I went on a mission. I slowly walked down the college dormitory hallway looking for the girls. Faintly, I heard some commotion in one of the rooms. I knocked lightly on the door and opened it with trepidation. As I rounded the corner, I saw my quiet and unassuming camp classmate crouched in a corner crying her eyes out. Turns out, that the two of the ringleaders partnered up to terrorize her. They were pointing at her and saying that she was dirty and nobody liked her. They were going on and on berating the girl and she was just losing it. Their words about her were not true, but they'd picked their target and there were no signs of an end.

At that moment, a switch flipped inside of me. At least seven other campers were witnessing this atrocity, yet, nobody was saying a thing. Nobody stood up for her, and I couldn't take it. I said, "Stop. She's none of those things. You have no right to say that about her. She didn't do anything to you." This girl was painfully shy, so they just picked her because she wasn't going to say anything back. Of course now the target moved from this girl to me, so I was staring at them and they shouted, "Backup. You're always in somebody's business." A Busy body: does that sound familiar? "You're always in somebody's business. This isn't your fight. Back up." I didn't back down. "This *is* my business. You don't have a right to treat people this way," I said. "I actually came to talk to you about this very thing."

We moved to the center of the room for more space and distance from my terrified friend. There, I was attempting to rationalize with the bullies. I told the main girl, Ashanti, "This is unacceptable. You can't treat people this way. It's not right!" I felt a tap on my left shoulder coming from behind. It was Bethany, the other bully. I didn't have time to be distracted. I was focused on Ashanti. Bethany would have to wait. The tapping on my shoulder continued. This girl wasn't going to give up, but I have a stubborn streak. I wasn't going to give in, but finally, I turned to Bethany. Maybe it was the Southern hospitality in me that couldn't continue to ignore her taps, so I turned to let her know that I was going to continue with Ashanti right now. Turning back to the elevated tone of Ashanti, I didn't anticipate what would happen next.

Suddenly, I felt my headscarf loosen and drop to the ground. My perfectly wrapped hair fell down into my eyes. Bethany was determined to get my attention. So determined that she pulled the scarf off of my head. I was shocked. Floored. Confused. Did this girl just touch my hair? Oh no, she didn't.

I thought, OK, I *have a couple choices right now. I could completely lose it because she has now touched my hair or I can stay focused.* I chose the middle ground, and I turned to Bethany who was right next to me breathing down my neck. I pushed her out of my personal space and away from my hair. I said, "Get off me. Don't touch me." I turned away one last time to continue this non-fruitful conversation with Ashanti, and BOOM, just like that my head swiveled to the right. I had been clocked right above my left eye. That's right. Bethany punched me. I'm not sure if you have ever experienced this, but I felt like I was living in a remake of *Mean Girls* meets a hood rap song.

How did it all happen so fast? I had pushed this girl, and she clocked me in the face. This was completely out of my character. I was the girl who gracefully walked the stages in pageants. I was the girl who danced. I was the girl who played piano. I surely was not the girl who participated in knock-down drag out fights, but here I was facing just that. Once I registered that I had just been hit, I thought to myself, *OK, I never considered being in this situation. I've never been in a fight before. I don't know if I can fight, but I feel like I should fight because I'm in a fight.*

I went back and forth in my head about what to do. *Should I strike back even though it was just one punch and a headscarf*

79

grab? If so, that's an actual fight. I had a sense that my parents would be supportive of me if I got one hit in due to self-defense. *Should I do nothing and then just see what happens? Should I engage in a full on, knock-her-down, drag her by her neck and pull her earrings out of her earlobes type of fight?* I didn't really know if she knew how to fight. I had those three options in my head and everybody in the room was in stunned silence at this point.

They wanted to see what I would do. I looked at her with fire of revenge in my eyes. After the punch, she walked far, far away from me. She didn't even look like she would get close to me out of fear and shock. Finally, I turned to her and said, "Did you just hit me?" Silence. Nobody said a thing. I looked her square in the eye with determination. I pointed right at her nose and I said, "You're going to pay." I had chosen the fourth option that I hadn't considered - to fight with my words and intellect. I pointed out that she needed to get some self-respect, boundaries, real friends, and some edges. (Just kidding about the edges part. That wasn't a trend yet.) Instead of cursing her out, I used some SAT level words that caused her to stutter in her retort. It wasn't one of my proudest moments, but I definitely won at hitting below the belt. I'd been in enough situations where I had to stand up for myself and all of those sassy moments from my past were used to perfection in this moment. I counted it as a win.

That evening I called my parents, let them know that I had just been in a fight, and that I was about to get kicked out of camp. I also told them that I would do it all again, if needed. They agreed and totally had my back. They understood what had happened and were (for the most part) proud of how I handled the situation. In the end, I stayed through the end of the camp (minus a day) and Bethany went home immediately.

While I may not be a world-class fighter, to this day, I refuse to stand by while I see people get bullied who are incapable of standing up for themselves. I feel the need to be their voice, and it was then that I realized I was wired for that. I can care less what other people say about me. I'm more concerned about those people who have a purpose, but they're too scared to do something about it. I'm going to step in and do what I need to do for them to see results. I'm going to intervene just like the busy body title that I was given in kindergarten. I have always fought for the little guy and I bring that same mentality to the workplace. When I see abuse in the workplace, I stand up against it. You are likely the same way about what you deem as injustice. You might have something in you that makes you angry, something that riles you up, and you will realize that it's a part of your purpose and personality that will guide you as you move forward.

Even now in my presentations, I speak to that person who doesn't feel like they have a voice at the moment. I empower that person so that they no longer feel like they are unable to experience joy and happiness. If you are on the fence about dreaming again and elevating your business, I encourage you to take a step towards your dream. I refuse to sit by and watch the big man, the bully, or the corporation be the only ones with access to the good life when there are so many talented, amazing people who are just too fearful to step in their dreams. I am called to the person who feels little right now, but in actuality, they are big.

The confidence that I displayed during the situation with those bullies was birthed through previous experiences. It came from being hazed on cheerleading squads and from falling and busting my behind (and face) while tumbling. That confidence came from every opposition that I had faced and risen above. When you review your past, you'll start to see all of those little things have laid a foundation for growth and maturity in a certain area. Now it's up to you to activate those truths in the best possible way. While I'm no professional fighter, I could lay hands if necessary.

Consider the moments that have shaped you, be them embarrassing, difficult, and mind-wrecking to the point where you fought to stay sane. Remember those moments and realize that every single experience is a building block for your dream.

seven

Step 4: Resurrect

A life without a dream and purpose is merely a lackluster, unfulfilling space of time. It barely qualifies as an existence.

Once you have reviewed your life and where you've come from, now it is time to resurrect the dream. Revisit the dream that has been lying dormant within you. It's time to give yourself permission to dream again.

As children, we are told that we can do anything, be anything, and go anywhere. We are told that the sky's the limit, and we can reach for the stars. Yet, simultaneously we received messages that encouraged us to pick something that we're good at, do what our parents say, and pursue what's appropriate. We're taught to stay in line and do what makes sense. Obviously, these are competing messages. One message emphasizes that anything is possible regardless. The other message says anything is possible within reason. Over time, "within reason" becomes smaller and more defined as something that has been done before and something that can be understood by most. This school of thought creates a pattern of doing things that are comfortable, familiar and expected.

Dream, Build, Repeat.

When this thought process becomes your new normal, but you strive to follow the "right" path and make the "right" decisions, you will find yourself coming up to a point of frustration. If you are truly a dreamer on the inside (which I know you are), if you truly are a rebel without a cause, if you're truly a person who has a passion to see lives changed, you will find it frustrating to be consistently pressured by other people's expectations. There is a path already laid out for you to be successful. You may have been told that you must go to school and major in a particular area in order for you to make a certain amount of money and experience a level of success.

Expectation is everywhere, but I want to challenge you to challenge the expectations. Challenge the expectations that society has placed on you. It's time to kick those expectations to the curb because it's time for you to take the limits off of yourself, put your focus on something larger than yourself, and reach for the thing that seems impossible. You'll accomplish that thing twenty times over.

The only way to experience authentic growth outside of expectation is to resurrect the dream that has been lying dormant inside of you. You'll know that this dream has been lying dormant because you have felt a level of restlessness throughout this book. You have felt the need to do something different and you're looking for tools and strategies to break out of this box that society has placed you in. That is how you know that you have a dream that's dormant inside of you. You know that you have a dream that's dormant inside of you because you have picked up this book. This book is your sign to tell you that it's time to stop editing yourself, forming, shaping, and molding yourself into this shell of a person that you don't even like, but everyone else loves.

It's time to wake that dream up. This chapter is focused on resurrecting your true, innate self so that you can bubble to the surface and amplify your life in a way that you have never experienced up until this point. To do this, you must give yourself permission to dream again.

The moment that you started to dream again is aligned with this book. For me, it was on social media. I know, it's such a millennial thing to say, but I'm forever grateful for social media for connecting me to incredible people! There I was, scrolling through my timeline and there was a picture of a woman who looked like she was living her absolute best life. She was vibrant, smiling, and owning the stage in front of a huge audience of people. The caption was intriguing about how someone had gone to this woman's event and been impacted and transformed. I scrolled to find out more about who this person was, what the event was, and how I could be there next time. You see, when I saw this post, something resonated within me that let me know I needed more. There was a familiarity in her posts that showed me something that was already within me waiting to be explored. As I read through her bio, I came to realize that it was not the first time that I had seen this woman.

In fact, when I was in middle school, I watched and rooted for her on television. I looked up to everything she stood for as a woman, an influencer, and a business owner. All of this led me to go onto her website, sign up for her email list because I needed to know the next time she would be having an event. The next time she did something, I needed to be there. There was something in my soul, the depths of my soul that looked at that profile, that picked up her writing, that looked at her videos. I said, "This person has something for me."

You see, I didn't need a sales pitch. I didn't need anyone to force this information down my throat, but as soon as I saw it, it resonated with me. I don't know if you've had that experience with someone. I hope that you have that experience with someone where you read their writing, you view their videos, you hear their story, and it connects with you and it begins to awaken something inside of you that you didn't even realize was still there. Her profile, her life, her ministry, if you will, spoke to me in such a way that it transformed how I began to see myself.

I want to pause here to emphasize the fact that she had no idea I was having this moment. All she did was be obedient to her call. She was in position to produce what she was passionate about and in the appropriate time, I found it. Don't you dare think that you can't have the same type of impact on someone. However, that only happens when you're in the flow of your dream and purpose.

In elementary school, I wanted to be a speaker and I didn't know that it was possible as a career field. I thought speakers had to be fancy famous people. I thought speakers had to have a particular schooling and education. I thought speakers had to have a certain amount of accolades. Within a year of this awakening, I had the opportunity to meet, get to know, and be mentored by this amazing woman that I found on the Internet.

Through that journey, I found that I too had a message that was life-giving. I had a message that I could share with someone that would possibly change their lives, and it was that moment when her life would change mine forever. She gave me permission to dream. She became my big sister and she spoke such life into me. She showed me what was possible and I became passionate about doing the same thing for others.

I submit to you this question: what is your dream? Have you had an idea in the back of your mind but you've felt too inadequate to pursue? You don't have to have the strategy yet. You don't have to have the provision yet, you simply need the idea to start. This is your time to name that dream. You have permission to dream again. You don't need approval or acceptance from anyone except yourself and God. That's it.

After this awakening, I became hypersensitive to those who had been silenced by life and began speaking to them. I envision these people. In the marketing world, we call this an archetype. It's the profile of the person that you're dedicated to helping. I could speak the language of those people because their stories were my story, my friend's story, or my family's story.

I began speaking to that girl crying in the bathroom because she was being bullied. I spoke to that girl who could barely get out of bed after losing a pageant because her worth was found in titles. I spoke to that guy who felt stuck pursuing a career because of family pressure. I spoke to that guy who put his ideas on the back burner because his past ideas were shot down.

My message became that there's life on the other side of rejection and the moment that you see the excellence within you, you will be able to press forward with confidence with or without the support of those around you.

I became passionate about working with thought leaders, creatives, dreamers, and consultants who know that there is something more outside of their nine-to-five jobs but do not know how to make the shift. I became passionate about working with entrepreneurs to clarify their messaging, attract their tribes, and serve with authenticity. I became passionate about calling out the gifts in others and encouraging them to pursue them fearlessly. I became passionate about speaking life, hope, and strategy into their lives, but it all began with a social media hashtag that sparked my interest. A hashtag started me on a path to work with a mentor that changed my life.

A hashtag gave me permission to dream again. Know that it doesn't have to be this earth-shattering moment, but it's a moment, nonetheless. Too often signs, confirmations, and inspirations are missed because they're brushed under the rug as insignificant. Or sometimes, we act like Gideon in the Bible and we need confirmation, after confirmation, after confirmation. Seeking repeated signs as proof that you're going down the right path is nothing more than doubt and indecision that only hinders your progress and potential. Seeking significant, specific signs before you take action, instead of trusting yourself, your guiding principles and/or your faith, further proves the need for you to do some work to cut out the blending and acceptance that you crave. Some transformation requires immediate action. If I had waited, watched, and pondered, I would have missed the opportunity to be mentored by an incredible coach. My journey would have been in a holding pattern because after that, she stopped accepting clients. Overthinking is not the way to see your dreams manifested, but quick, prudent, action is. To top it off, confirmation is also found along the journey, not just before you start.

However, even with encouragement and the mindset that something else was possible for my life, I was still unclear about what I personally had to offer. After all, after years of viewing yourself in one light, it takes time to reprogram and see yourself as a new, refined being. After banging my head against the wall for a bit, I began to do a dream dump. A dream dump is the idea of writing down everything that you find interesting or intriguing. It might include a massive amount of random words, it might be a list, it might be a statement of what you want your life to look like. The dream dump is the time where you put down everything that you could possibly want, everything that you could possibly enjoy, like in personal life, business strategy, anything. You just put that on paper. The toughest part about doing this exercise is the temptation to self-edit. Self-editing limits creativity and masquerades itself as realism. It removes creativity and freedom by showering your biggest dreams in doubt, questions, and limitations. An example from my dream dump is the idea of traveling full-time and becoming a digital nomad (someone who can live and work anywhere with Internet and electricity). Self-editing questions the finances, the family questions, and the opinions of friends. It's a small-minded perspective from your not-so-distant past.

After the dream dump, the next step in your process of awakening and discovering the dream inside is to ask others. Ask trusted colleagues, family members, and friends the following questions.

1. What do you think I'm good at?

2. If you could create the perfect job for me, what elements would it include?

3. How have I helped or impacted you?

4. If you had to describe me in three words, what would they be and why?

5. When you think of what skills I bring to the table, what would you say?

Most likely you'll be surprised what your colleagues, friends, and family members say about you. As you ask these questions, they will likely begin to call out things that you never realized were unique and special. You never realized you had these characteristics because they came so naturally to you that you didn't even think of them as being a skill or something that assisted anyone else. In fact, that's a hint to know that something is a part of your purpose and it could be a path to executing your big dream. Compare this list with the list you created, and start visualizing what your life could look like if you were to pursue your dream.

Competing voices

I was coaching a college senior, Chloe, from college to life transition. She found me after I spoke at her university and knew that she needed to work with me. She shared that she was stuck between three differing opinions regarding her post-graduation life. She had people telling her that she needed to graduate and get a job because that was the entire point of going to college. She had professors telling her that she should pursue graduate school because she had so much potential, but she just needed to hone in on a specialty in the career they saw for her. Finally, she had her own idea, something she was incredibly passionate about, but was terrified to pursue. She dreamed of working in videography and photography. She had never seen it done before and wasn't really excited to live a broke-artist's lifestyle. During our time working together, she told me about a retreat that she went to where people were asked to submit words about her. Each person at this retreat was asked to provide kind words of encouragement to each other and others, like me, were asked to submit a letter as well. At the end, they were provided with letters of affirmation and truth. Chloe shared how transformational it was to hear how other people saw her. It shifted her mindset and perspective for the better. The same thing would go for you. This idea of soliciting feedback from others has the potential to transform how you show up for other people. In fact, it might further confirm how the way you see yourself can be vastly different than how people see you.

To sum up Chloe's story, she chose to bet on her skills and interests. We laid out a plan with services that she could offer, a strategy to access clients with budgets, and clarified what made her stand out from the competition. Now, she's the proud owner of a creative studio that provides branding photography and videography services. She was able to accomplish this in her early twenties because she took immediate action to align herself with someone who had results in the area she was seeking. This step caused her to resurrect that little idea in the back of her heart and she dedicated herself to sharing her dream with the world.

Identifying the truth

My friend Ayisha is a ghostwriter. More than that, she's a writer at her core. She always has a notebook to jot down ideas, revelations, and anything else that comes to mind, and it's been like this since I met her. She essentially writes an essay every time she opens her notebook. I don't relate to that at all, even though I strive to be that kind of person. I barely journal and have countless unfinished notebooks. It's just not really my thing. Ayisha says there's something within writers that prompts them to record information in the moment. I was having dinner with her and she was telling me how she started her entrepreneurial journey and asked me if I was a writer. Of course, I told her no. I clearly didn't fit the profile that she described and the conversation continued to flow. Two hours into the conversation, I casually mentioned that I had operated a blog for years. She stared at me dumbfounded and utterly confused about why I told her that I wasn't a writer. I downplayed it and said that I didn't blog daily like I used to, and it's not that big of a deal, just a few thoughts here and there. She gave me the side eye and told me that I was definitely a writer. I refuted her again.

We continued our conversation and I casually mentioned that I'm on a content marketing team responsible for blogging, writing email sequences, sales pages, and social media content. Not surprisingly, she looked at me with that same dumbfounded look and emphasized the fact that I declined the title of writer again. I let her know that I wasn't a writer. I just happened to write a few emails and posts for a six-figure online business launch.

At that point, she basically slapped me upside the head and said, "Casey, you're a writer." It seems obvious now, especially as I write this, but at the time, I couldn't get it through my mind. I didn't see myself in that way, and I didn't fit the profile of what I believed a writer to be. I simply saw myself as someone who would jot down information, who could write a quick blog, and who could synthesize a client's idea into language that would resonate with their ideal audience.

As I continued down my path of clear denial, I had to think back to my writing experiences, pre-entrepreneurship. At six years old, I decided to try my hand at writing a story. After all, I loved reading and it was time to get some fresh content. I pulled out this hunk of metal that they called a laptop in the 1990s and started on my idea. I was writing a story about a good witch, because I felt the good should be seen in everyone. Naturally, my family was horrified that as a young, impressionable kid in a Christian household I would be interested in writing a story about a "good" witch. I tried to explain that everyone says that witches are bad, but there must be good ones. I was trying to rewrite the narrative. It was less about the actual witch and more about someone who was misunderstood. I saw someone in society, if you will, a witch, who always got the bad rap. I saw her and I wanted to change the narrative and say, *just because that's what people say about you, that's not who you are.* I wanted to change the narrative and make her a good witch who helped people because she was kind, but because I grew up in a very good, loving, Christian environment, I was told that my story wasn't appropriate and that it should not be told. That was the last time I ever wrote a creative piece. Essentially this character was just a nice person and it could have been written as such, but you know, the creative process of a six-year-old isn't fully developed yet. Just to emphasize here, I don't blame anyone for this experience, but you never know what impacts you and how.

This experience was likely why I could never really get out of the structured environment of only writing for class. I thought, *I'm not an actual writer, because clearly, I'm not talented because I wasn't able to complete that story of the good little witch.* It seems so small and minute, but situations that happened in your past still impact you. There are things that people have spoken over you that simply were not true, but they are impacting how you operate today. They are also impacting how you see yourself today. So even as I'm writing this book, I still struggled to see myself as a writer, but because a positive colleague friend of mine said I was a writer, I had to look at the fruit and say, "Yes, I am a writer!" You never know how someone else's words can push you toward or away from your dream and destiny.

Regardless of your past experiences, there's a cost associated with not following the thing that you were created to do. You may not see the cost right now, but there are people who are dying and perishing on the inside because you have not stepped into your full dream. You have not yet awakened to the dream that's deep inside of you because of fear. You haven't awakened to that dream inside of you because you feel like you're unqualified. Maybe you haven't awakened to the dream inside of you because someone else hasn't stepped into their purpose, but guess what? This is activation season, and there is a cost of not pursuing your dream.

My spiritual journey was very similar to how I found my mentor. I read a blog post that totally changed my perspective on faith. Suddenly, the Christianity that I was indoctrinated in that had become this abstract faith thing had now been explained in a way that I could understand it, and it convicted me to my soul. I no longer had the excuse that I didn't understand. I no longer had the excuse that they weren't speaking my language. All excuses were removed. I knew that I am great in God's eyes. All of my excuses and barriers were removed, because I read a post from a person who had been obedient to her calling. Today I often wonder where I would be in my business or spiritual journey had those two women (my mentors) not stepped up and followed the dreams that were placed inside of them? I definitely would not be coaching men and women to a place of transformation.

There are people who are attached to your "yes." There are people who are associated with your personal, professional, and spiritual growth. There are people who are associated with the dream that's inside of you. The longer you decide to sit on your dream, the longer people will be stuck in their ways. The longer you decide to push off all the signs, the longer you decide that you're not good enough. There are people who are struggling, and they will not step out of their struggle until you step into your dream. However, if you refuse, if you continue on this path of personal frustration and you continue to stuff the dream down deeper and deeper inside of you, you will continue to ignore the tugs at your heart. You better believe that there will eventually be someone else who will be raised up to do what you wanted to do, but I hope and I pray that you don't allow that to happen. I hope and pray that as you read these words, something is stirring on the inside of you, that something is awakening and activating you. Even now, there are ideas that are coming to your mind. Even now as you're reading this, the ideas are confirming where you need to go. Don't discount the small idea. Don't discount the vague fragment of an idea that may or may not be something big. Write it down and declare it. Think on it and grow it, because progress starts with just a seed of an idea.

It starts with a seed and that's what that social media post was for me. That was a seed and I began to water that seed with content. I began to water that seed with prayer. I began to water that seed with mentorship. I began to water that seed with action. I began to water that seed with activation, and all of a sudden, I had a harvest full of a dream that I never even realized was on the inside of me. But without identifying that seed and confirming that there is something there, I would still feel frustration. I would still feel that tug. Have you ever been in that position where you've seen something that someone else was doing, and you instantly identified it as something you could be doing? There's a level of urgency that is in this season right now. As soon as you have an idea, there is a level of action that is required to activate that thing.

So as you are getting these dream ideas, realize that your time is now. If you have an idea, if you have a dream, part of that dream is to come to pass right now. It might not be coming to pass in full today because growth and maturation need to happen, but there is a seed and as long as you plant that seed of a dream, now with urgency, you will begin to see the fruit of it. People are waiting on you. People are waiting on you to step in to the place that you were created to occupy. Your future is waiting on you. Your dream is important. Your passion is important. Your life is important. It's time to resurrect the person, the dream, the desire that has been deep inside of you, awaken it, and act on it. Don't fear. Your time is now.

eight

Step 5: Refuse

Opposition and resistance are side effects of an activated dream; refuse to let them take you out.

As soon as you decide that your dream is worth something, that your voice is valuable, and your passion has purpose, you will begin to experience a level of opposition. It may start out small, or it may start out big, but regardless, opposition will come and it's there to distract you from action. Opposition's goal is to take your eyes off the dream and put your eyes on the situation. Its goal is to keep you stuck, stagnant, and frustrated. For this stage of dreaming and building and executing, you must refuse to fall victim to the following opposition tactics.

1-Lack of Urgency

We've already talked about how there is a grace on diligent speed and there are people tied to your passion, your dream, and your purpose. These people are physically and figuratively unable to move forward until you get into position. I was unable to become a mentee of a mentor who had not stepped up into a mentorship role.

97

I was unable to join a program that was not offered. I was unable to access a teacher's ideas that hadn't made it into a structured process and product. Transformation occurs through alignment of positioning and timing. Both require urgency.

There are people who want to work with you, but you do not have the structure, strategy, and plan in place in order to receive them yet. There are people who need to learn from your leadership, but you are hesitant to go for the promotion even though you are over-qualified. There are people waiting to see themselves in you, but you are committed to waiting for just the right moment… that never comes.

Don't think that you have all day, all year, or all lifetime to start, because you don't. Your time is now. Sound familiar? It seems to be a theme, doesn't it? Refuse to believe the lie that there is an unlimited amount of time, because we all know that it's not true. Don't allow time to pass by with this dream awakened, but stagnant, inside of you. It's up to you to act and it's up to you to act expeditiously.

2-Perfectionism

There were countless times where I came up with a business name, a business idea, a mission statement, colors, blogs, ideal target audiences and everything for my next great thing. I would get ready to launch, and then I would decide that an edit was needed here and there. The edits would take on a life of their own and slowly, unintentionally, I would start the process again. Questioning the name of this business, the people, the message, the results. All of it. Amongst all of the changes, the idea would get lost in a file for later when the timing was better.

The foundation that I laid would be ripped up, reworked, laid down, and ripped up again – never having the opportunity to nurture and mature through execution and feedback. If you continuously rip up a foundation that is not in need of repair, you will never build on top of it. You will constantly stay at the ground level over and over and over again. While you look busy, like you're hustling, your perfectionism is keeping you from your clients and your promotion. Your perfectionism is doing nothing other than boosting up your pride and putting yourself up on a pedestal. As you have elevated yourself to this pedestal of perfection, which is completely impossible to attain, your dream is still not being activated. Your perfectionism is a way for you to attempt to control the uncontrollable. Let's have a truth moment: perfectionism almost kept me from completing this book. I was so fearful that people wouldn't like the book or that it wouldn't meet whatever standard I imagined existed. Know that perfection can never be attained and it is just another form of fear manifesting in a widely accepted form.

3- Fear of Failure or Fear of Success

We talked about how perfectionism is a form of fear already, but there is also fear associated with failure. It's the idea that if I put an imperfect concept out into the world, I will be ripped apart. *No one will purchase my product. No one will come to my event. I will be broke. Everyone will laugh at me, and I will just stay here.* Honestly, you will begin to feel like the world is better without your idea. This is an example of fear of failure. Hear this truth. Nobody cares. Not what you expected, but true nonetheless. Social media doesn't care that your product was a flop. Why? Because they forgot about what you posted on your timeline. They saw your one post, thought it was cute, and kept scrolling. Maybe it's not that your product doesn't make sense. It could be that you don't know who you're serving. Maybe it's not the fact that your concept is not a good concept. Maybe it's the fact that your fear of failure has kept you from putting yourself out there enough to encourage people to take action. Alternatively, fear of success causes you to downplay your accomplishments. You begin to downplay what your business has accomplished. You begin to downplay the results that you've gotten on the projects that you've worked on. You neglect to tell your boss what you've done and the impact you've made on the team and organization as a whole. Your fear of success also keeps your career, income, and position stagnate. Both fear of success and fear of failure will keep you from walking into the completion of your dream.

4- Unforgiveness of Past Experiences

We've talked about the importance of reviewing your past, but the key component of reviewing anything that was painful is the act of forgiveness. It's not to harp on those things that happen. You review them, partly, to simply acknowledge that they happened and now take that negative experience and flip it to a positive and say, "I forgive that person for talking about me. I forgive that person for labeling me. I forgive that boss for not promoting me. I forgive that parent for speaking negativity over me instead of speaking life over me." You begin to look at those negative past experiences through a lens of forgiveness, and now you see it with pure, clear eyes instead of a skewed perspective, due to unforgiveness. You'll begin to see that negativity in your future as well, so until you change your perspective, until you acknowledge that your past can be forgiven, you'll be unable to fully move into where you want to be (and do it with a pure heart). To move forward, you need to forgive and heal from your past experiences. It seems so small. It seems minor to forgive even the teacher who labeled you or mislabeled you, but as soon as you do that, there's a level of clarity that will come from knowing the truth and deciphering truth from lies.

5- Family and Friends

Some people around you don't want to see you hurt and they take it upon themselves to keep you safe. These people project their fear and their past negative experiences and failures onto you. Others truly don't want to see you succeed. Either way, if you are experiencing negativity or lack of support from family and friends, it's time to start distancing yourself while you're in this fresh place of inspiration. Begin to look for a community of entrepreneurs, faith walkers, corporate mentees, and colleagues who will support you rather than tear you down in this vulnerable state and season. I'm not telling you to kick everyone from your upbringing to the curb, but I am saying that your dream is sensitive. It's like your newborn baby. New mothers are advised to keep newborns away from the outside world for at least six weeks. Why? For their immune systems. During infancy, their bodies need a chance to build up the strength to fight off everything that doesn't belong. A baby doesn't have the ability to fight. This is often what happens with dreams. Sometimes we have put our baby dream out into the world and people have come against it and they've come to fight it, and we didn't have enough strength or power to fight back. So we just allowed our little dream baby to die because we exposed it to the elements. We exposed it to negativity and pessimism while it was just too young.

That is not what I want for your dream baby. I want your dream baby to be surrounded by love, support, health, and strength. And that only comes from a network of people who can build you and your dream up when you need it. Don't think that you can do this walk alone. That's why I wrote this book. I wrote this book so you can have a manual to say that t*his is how I can accomplish the dream.* I wrote this book so that you know that you're not alone, and I wrote it for a community of people who know that there's more to life than what they're experiencing right now. I want you to find those people who believe with you.

6- Comfort

Your level of comfort is keeping your dream from coming to fruition. Have you decided that your television binge is more important than your dream? Have you decided that happy hour is more lit than your passion? Have you decided that leaving work early and showing up late to work is more important than that promotion that you have wanted? It's all about choices, and you can either choose to be comfortable and stay in the exact same place where you are or you can choose to be uncomfortable by making decisions that may confuse or upset people. Choose to put your dream to the forefront because your dream matters. Your level of comfort, your level of excitement, of sleep, it all matters. Sleeping in and then going to bed early will get in the way of your dream execution. However, you must decide to sacrifice sometimes in order for your dream to come to fruition. A sacrifice must be made. A sacrifice of time, finances, of your comfort. Furthermore, once you decide that your comfort is not as important as your dream, you will see unimaginable levels of productivity and fruit from your willingness to grind. Know that this process or "hustle-mode" won't last forever. It's a season while you're building and taking action for the transformation of your tribe.

Often we think that people just wake up and they're an overnight success, but I can almost guarantee that there were some times when they put in late nights and early mornings, sacrificed sleep, a television show, or social media time in order to lay the foundation for their dreams. As soon as it caught fire, they moved forward with ease. They were accelerated and no one could understand their "quick" acceleration, but they knew it was because they sacrificed their comfort. They decided that laziness was no longer welcome in their life and they began to see fruit from their dream.

7- Negative Self Talk

Negative self-talk is what you say in the mirror to yourself in the comfort of your bathroom. It's the talk that you use to degrade your physical features. You may think, "Why do I look like this? Why does my hair do this? Why doesn't my beard connect?" Your self-talk may also be about your skills and talents. Maybe you compare: Why don't I have the tech skills of that person down the street?

Why can't I speak as eloquently as him? Why don't I have the business insight she has?

You begin to look at everybody else's life and you compare yours to theirs. You compare yourself to them. You compare your skills to theirs. That narrative gets played over and over and over again. It crowds out every positive thought that you've ever had while becoming a broken record of negativity in your mind. You're now meditating on those negative things, and as you meditate on the negativity, you begin to manifest the negativity. Your brain follows what your mind says, and your mind follows what your heart feels.

If you feel like a failure, you will begin to manifest actions and activities of a failure. Conversely, if you meditate on positive things, if you begin to affirm yourself, you will look in the mirror each morning and say, "I am fabulous. I am fearfully and wonderfully made. I am handsome. I love the way that my beard and mustache do not connect. I love the way that I have a little extra fluff. I love that I am creative. I love that I am unique and different and special," and as you affirm those things about yourself, that's what you will begin to meditate on. As you're meditating on the fact that you are a winner, you begin to act as a winner. Winners walk with confidence. You will walk with boldness, because after all, you know that you are amazing, and you will begin to manifest amazing things.

Your thoughts have power. I recall an example of how I will constantly call someone a friend in my head. I'll follow them on social media. I'll read their content, and I'll be inspired by them, and somehow, in the past, I have ended up meeting many of these people. I end up in the same space with these people. Why?

Step 5: Refuse

Because I manifested it. I meditated on positivity. I supported what they were doing. I took action when an opportunity presented itself, and I meditated on winners' actions. It's less about who the person is and more about the concepts of positive thinking and support. It's about following through on something that inspires you. So instead of meditating on the negativity, begin to meditate on the positive things. As you work your way through these seven points and realize that you have done them, move with urgency to create change. Instead of being a perfectionist, become a doer. Instead of having a fear of failure or success, walk in boldness. Instead of harboring unforgiveness about past experiences, forgive and move on. Instead of surrounding yourself with negativity from family members and past friends, find a community of support. When you decide that your laziness and comfort isn't as important as results and diligence, decide that you're going to replace the negative talk with positive self-talk. You will then see that your dreams will not only come to fruition, but they will come to fruition quickly because you have now activated positive habits. You will see positive fruit from positive action. So anytime you experience any of those seven negative feelings, thoughts, or actions, make a conscious effort to replace them with positivity. Make a conscious decision to decide that you are no longer going to focus on those negative things, but you are going to throw the negative away. You're going to dispose and discard of that negativity and you're going to fill the negative voids with positivity. That is how you will begin to see your dream come to fruition.

Dream, Build, Repeat.

nine

Step 6: Run

***Follow-through is what separates the mediocre
from the extraordinary.***

A dream without execution is like those fabulous shoes that stay in the back of your closet because they hurt your feet. You know they're valuable, but completely pointless. No one gets to see how fabulous and fly they are because they sit in the back of your closet gathering dust. You gaze at them with love and adoration, but you also remember the pain. Therefore no one gets to see them again. That's how your dream is neglected when it is not executed. It's time to execute and activate your dream.

Your journey does not stop when you uncover your dream. That's really the beginning of your journey. Don't merely talk about the dream, you must embody the dream. It becomes your lifestyle. You begin to breathe life into it.

You might not have all of the pieces together, but you must start. The best example that I can ever find about someone who started before they had all the pieces together, someone who decided that they were going to say "yes" before they had the full plan is this guy named Noah. I love this story because it's a perfect picture of what it looks like to move by faith, to move without a full plan, to move with just a God idea and a drive and motivation. The story of Noah is found in the book of Genesis in the Bible. Noah was a guy living his best life, minding his own business until one day he gets this message that it is time for him to pivot. It was time for him to do something a little bit different, which turns out to be this crazy idea from God asking him to build an ark.

God reportedly told him that he needed to build this big boat for an insane amount of rain that would come in the future. It would be so much rain that the whole world would be washed away and only the people and animals that would be on that boat will be saved. To us that doesn't sound like such a crazy request. Well, the part about the whole world being washed away, it's pretty crazy, but the idea that a lot of rain would come or that a boat was needed is not that crazy. However, up until this point, there's no evidence that they had ever seen rain, so we can speculate that at this point, he doesn't even really know what rain is. We can speculate that he doesn't really know what a boat is. We can speculate that he definitely doesn't know what an ark is considering that an ark is just a boat on major steroids, yet he received this message and he decided that he would follow it no matter how crazy it seemed. Now, Noah was working on this ark for over fifty years. 5-0. Can you imagine working on your dream piece-by-piece, day-by-day, minute-by-minute for fifty years or more and not seeing it come to pass? Do you love the dream so much that you would consistently build and work even when you don't see success?

Are you able to consider a dream that is so beyond your imagination and so beyond your purview that you would commit your entire life to seeing the dream come to pass? Even in Noah's case, the circumstances around the situation did not seem conducive for this ark. That much rain had never fallen. Everything around him seemed to be opposed to the dream and the vision that he received, but the most important thing that we have to remember about this story and about your life is that the dream was given to Noah. The dream was not given to his wife, his children, to his boss, to his friends, or anyone else, for that matter. It was given to Noah. You may face opposition when people don't understand why you're so passionate. They may not understand why you're so in love with this bold, new idea. They don't get why you want to leave your job behind and pursue this concept full time. They don't understand why you went to school so long to become a doctor or your profession of choice. They don't understand, but guess what? It's not for them to understand. The dream is yours to hold onto. I think the reason that Noah was able to hold on for fifty plus years was because he knew where the dream came from. If you know that the dream came from a higher and greater place than you, you can simply become the vessel or the conduit for the dream to come to fruition. It's not even about you. So when the opposition comes, the opposition doesn't come for you. It comes for the dream, but the dream isn't you. You're simply a vessel of the dream.

It took a long time. He wasn't able to experience any level of public success for years, but guess what? He was not distracted by the timeline of his life. Today, it's easy to get distracted due to constant connection. You see people thriving at different levels and you begin to compare your dream, your timeline, your execution to other people's dream, timeline, and execution. You see that they started a business on Monday and on Friday they have now grossed over a million dollars in sales (because you know we have to post our sales on social media). Now you're looking at your business and your bank account wondering where the funds are. You're comparing your investment to that of another person's. Yet Noah wasn't deterred by his timeline and you shouldn't be either. Stop comparing your timeline to everyone else's timeline. It's *your* timeline, so no matter what your path of execution looks like, as long as you are executing consistently, there is no need to compare your success to anyone else's. When it was time for the ark to be completed it was completed. When it is your time to be promoted, you will be promoted. When it is your time for your business to blow up, it will. When it's time for your work to be recognized by a promotion, you will be promoted. It all goes back to alignment.

Obsessing about everyone else's success or failures is not going to speed up your progress, process, or timeline of success. However, Noah was diligent in the building of this idea God gave him. Stay diligent. It's easy to start out on fire to begin moving forward, and then over time that fire begins to fizzle until all of a sudden you're back to where you started. You still have that dream, but oh goodness, it's so exhausting and instead of executing the dream, now the dream has gone up on the shelf, and you decide that you're going to come back to it next week, next month, next quarter, or next year. Need I remind you that there are people who will drown without the ark of your dream?

When it finally rained, fifty plus years after he began to build the ark, Noah was ready. This is a powerful, powerful statement. When it rained, he was ready. For those of you who are building businesses, when the clients come, do you have someplace for them to go? When your video goes viral, do you have products ready for the people to purchase? For those of you in corporate, when the time comes for the executive to notice your work, is there some work to be noticed? Are you going to be ready when it rains? It's guaranteed to rain, but you want to have a space to accept the blessings and the overflow. Moreover, that only comes from diligent, consistent execution, so just like Noah, now isn't the time to be rational. It's time to dedicate your whole being, your whole soul, your whole mind, everything you have to this dream, and sometimes it gets a little confusing because you had this fragment of a dream, but guess what? Clarity comes with consistent action. Clarity comes with consistent action. I had to repeat it for those in the back.

Too often we try to make brand names and brand colors and brand identities with what we feel like people want. I see this so often as a brand strategist. Yet and still, until you start serving people, you don't have the full amount of clarity. You won't really know the skills that are needed to do that job because clarity comes through action, so instead of fretting on everything being perfect, start where you are. Start with the skills that you have right now. Start with the resources that you have right now, and as you continuously grow, move, and develop, you will become more and more clear about what you should be doing and what comes naturally to you, but clarity comes through consistent action. You must have an immovable amount of dedication to your dreams because your future, your tribe's future depends on it. I know it's easy for you to say that it's selfish, but it's not selfish. It's actually self-less for you to put your dream above yourself. That is a level of sacrifice that will elevate, grow, and develop you, and it will also serve others. Your dream has a dual benefit —for you and others.

Dream, Build, Repeat.

After coaching with personal branding clients, mentoring teens, writing for small businesses, and marketing for events, I realized that there really is a difference between complainers and doers. I can hear someone say that they want assistance or that they want support, and I can tell who's a complainer and who's a doer. How? A complainer is someone who wants to vent. They want to say all of the things that they see in the industry. They want to complain about all the changes that should happen, but when it comes time for them to act, they don't want to give up their lifestyle. They don't want to give up a little bit of time on the weekends to build their side hustle. They don't want to give up the comfort in their office space and put in a little bit more work to gain a new skill in order to be prepared to serve that need. They just want to complain.

However, doers are people who complain and say, "This market is outdated." They say that "taxis are a thing of the past, and, *hey, I have this new idea where I think I can create a taxi company from my phone and totally disrupt the market.*" They complained about an antiquated system and they changed it. They did something about it. You can complain that there are no people who look like you at an executive level and then you can decide that you are going to pave the way to be a trailblazer in that industry. You can do something about it or you can go create a hashtag on social media and think that you did something, however one hashtag does not equate to transformation. It's simply a start. Are you a doer or are you a complainer? Are you a doer? Are you a complainer? That's an honest question. I won't judge you either way. You just have to know who you are at the moment.

I personally enjoy working with doers. I enjoy working with people who say that there is something that needs to change about

112

Step 6: Run

society. There's something that needs to change about business. There's something that needs to change, and they decide they're going to do something about it. That's why I created the Dream Disciple Movement™.

What does it mean to be a dream disciple? That means that you have a vision and dream, and you are a disciple of it. That means you follow it whole-heartedly. That means you have sacrificed everything to see this dream come to fruition. That's the definition of a dream disciple, and I am calling you. If you are reading this book, you have the potential to be a dream disciple, someone who decided that their future life could be different based on today's execution of the dream.

It's time to run. It's time to run fast after your dreams. It's time to be a dream disciple. Dream disciples live a *sorry, not sorry,* unapologetic lifestyle. That means that if you are reading this book, you are unapologetic to be who you are. I hope that you feel empowered enough to take the thing that comes naturally to you and spread it with the world because the world needs your voice. The world needs your drive, your desire, your expertise, and your skillset. Are you on board? Use #DreamDiscipleMovement and #DreamBuildRepeat on social media or send an email to Hello@CaseySharperson.com and let me know that you're chasing down your dream. I have a special gift for those who do so!

Lastly, when you're running after this dream, you'll realize that you don't actually have time to focus on what other people are doing. You can only focus on what's ahead of you. In elementary, middle, and high school, I ran track. My events were the 100-meter, 200-meter, and occasionally the 4 x 100m relay. However, during my junior year, I found my groove in the high jump. I stand a whopping 5 feet and 3 inches tall. Not the ideal candidate for a jumper, but I've always appreciated being different and shifting perspectives. I was an excellent high jumper in my high school region and I always loved how the tall competitors would not see me as competition until I jumped higher than them. In fact, I earned a medal in my region before heading to the South Carolina State Qualifier. (Insert underdog mental toughness here.)

One thing that I learned about running sprints, especially in a relay is it's very, very strategic. There is only a short amount of time that you're allowed to look around you and that's basically at the start of the race. At the start of the race, you're looking to see how that first leg goes. You're looking at that first one hundred meters to see how that first person races. You're looking at that handoff and at the passing of the baton. When it's your turn, the only thing that you are focused on is your lane and that baton. There's a split second where you make eye contact when that baton hits your hand and you're off. You go straight, and you don't look around. You don't try to assess whether another runner is next to you. Your only focus is the finish line. You're not even focused on listening to the feet that are behind you, beside you, or in front of you. Your focus is ahead because the moment when you move your eyes, you lose traction, you lose speed, and you lose the race.

As an unapologetic dream disciple, you're not focused on other people. You're simply focused and committed to your dream, so run fast after the execution of your dream, and don't be like that cute pair of shoes that's hidden. Don't let your dream be that thing that sits up on a shelf untouched because you refuse to step out and execute it.

ten

Step 7: Receive

A dream in motion will attract abundance and provision.

Your dream is attractive and magnetic. Furthermore, living your dream makes you infinitely more attractive as a person. You'll notice that as you begin to flow in your gifts and flow into the divine assignment that you were created for, people will then become attracted to you. They'll begin to move towards you and recognize that there's something different and unique about you. They'll start inquiring about your process, your progress, and your track record. Relationally, you'll also probably notice that former flames and exes will begin to find you, by some odd miracle, and reach out to you. You'll find that people you never expected to follow and reach out to you will do so. You'll find that if you're single people will start sliding into your inboxes. If you're married, the same might happen. They can't help it. Purpose, dreams, alignment, and flow are attractive.

As you get more and more comfortable running after your dream, you will become even more clear about your messaging. As a result, people will become clearer about what they ask of you.

For example, I was asked to work on a content team for this large launch. If you're not familiar, a launch is simply just sharing or putting out a new product, service, or event. Originally, the CEO and founder of the company reached out to me to inquire about me being a content writer. I applied and was accepted to a team of about twenty people. I completed the work early and on-time with excellence and was active as a part of this team. Then, my work and work ethic stood out from the crowd and was noticed by the CEO. As a result, I was asked to take lead of the content writers. Why? Because I consistently added value. Let's note that this was an unpaid opportunity. While I don't advocate for working for free forever, I am an advocate of strategic partnerships. I am also an advocate of being open to new opportunities and relationships. This opportunity came just after I discovered that I was a writer. Funny how that happens. I was flowing in communication. I was flowing in leadership. Due to that, I became attractive to move into this other role.

From that one, unpaid opportunity I have received multiple paid opportunities within this organization and others. I've been brought in as a clarity coach to work with their clients to clarify their message, encourage them, and provide strategic insight for quick results. I've seen businesses start, grow, thrive, pivot, become profitable, and influential because of this "yes." This was the evidence of becoming a dream disciple. I was going to take opportunities that gave me space to encourage, to uplift, to educate. I was committed to accept opportunities that matched the vision. You'll also find that the more you move and flow, the more that people may stretch you to do something that you've never done before.

As you begin to radiate in this flow, there will be elements of perceived competition. You're not in this marketplace alone. I'm not in this marketplace alone. There will always be another speaker. There will always be another writer. There's always someone else's book that you could have picked up. There's always someone else just as qualified or more qualified on paper than you. The difference between our perspective of competition and everyone else's is that we as readers of this book, are not going to be afraid of the competition. You realize that you were unique, special, gifted, and you dominate your area of expertise and when you dominate your area of expertise, there is no true competition. There are people who are going to be attracted to you. They are attracted to the way that you speak. They're attracted to your southern twang or your shared experiences. They're attracted to your story or your journey. While technically there's competition, there's also technically no competition due to your uniqueness.

A few years ago, I was working as an affiliate marketing manager for a six-figure grossing online launch. I was responsible for gathering up people who could help get the message out about this new product and service to the public. I was shocked by the number of influencers that I reached out to who responded back saying they only promote things that their faces were a part of. I understand that everyone has varying levels of capacity, but this idea goes back to strategic partnerships. They had no idea of the amount of potential that there was for them to have their faces a part of future projects and events. Because I had additional information and I understand the power of relationships, I saw how ego caused the loss of upside financial potential. Some were so concerned with experiencing competition that they missed alignment of their dream.

Never be afraid of being in the background or of operating from a place of support, rather than the forefront. There might be times where your dream calls you to do something in the background and people have no idea that you were even associated with it. I can guarantee that accepting certain opportunities that are aligned, whether your name is in front or your name is behind, are opportunities for growth, relationships, and a practice in humility. I think too often we as speakers, influencers and world changers are also attention seekers. We want to be on flyers, but we don't want to do any work to support other missions. Instead of viewing other organizations and other people as competition, view them as partners. View an opportunity to be in the background as an opportunity to partner with something and to elevate your dream in the background.

There's no competition when everyone is operating in their dream. I love spending time with other speakers, writers, strategists and coaches. I love associating with people who do the exact same thing that I do because I know that they do it differently than I do. I know that I have a secret sauce. Guess what? You do too! You have a secret sauce also. There can be two exact people, exact same experience, exact same services, but Group A will choose this person and Group B the other. They do that because each respective person reminds them of someone. Person B speaks in a language that they understand. Person A has understood the struggle. Person B has told their life story and they can relate to that.

People are attracted to authenticity. When you give freely, you will receive freely. When you are open to give of yourself, your services, your expertise and your skills, you will then be open to this reciprocal process to receive freely. You only get that when you're not afraid of the competition and you instead embrace the competition.

You'll realize when you're radiating in this dream space that your relationships and your reputation will speak for you. Metrics and followers might cause you to focus solely on likes over impact. Authenticity leaves when the sole focus is *who's going to see it* and not getting the message out ASAP. You might wonder if your boss noticed all of the work you did in that presentation. Did they hear that client rave about you? The truth is, there will be a period of time when it seems like you're grinding and nobody notices. Know this, people are watching. You would be surprised who is watching. The question here is, "How do you show up when you feel like nobody is watching?" How do you deliver at work when nobody is checking your timesheet? How do you deliver when nobody is reviewing your content? In the past, I haven't shared my marketing and corporate services on my website. Yet, clients have sought me out based on referrals. They seek me out based on emails that I've sent or based on relationships that I have. I know because these services are referral only. Again, you never know who's watching. You never know who's looking for what you offer. When you're consistently serving and doing what you do at a high level and you're executing well, then it doesn't matter who's watching or who's not watching, because this thing is reciprocal. If you produce positivity, diligence, and creativity, you'll experience the same. If you support other people's businesses by sending referrals, you will then start to receive referrals. When you nominate people for awards, people will do so for you in return and in due time, you will experience the law of sowing and reaping (reciprocity). Your reputation and your relationships will always speak for you.

The next way that you will radiate and execute is through your authenticity. When you are authentic to who you are, you will naturally begin to attract the right people to you because people won't receive any type of transformation from the person that you pretend to be.

There has to be a consistent challenge for you to tell people how you actually feel, not just what's acceptable. There has to be a challenge to show your vulnerability in your business, in your work, in your experiences. It's different. Everyone is used to a facade and a level of fakeness that when there is a smidge of authenticity, it is automatically intriguing. I challenge you to challenge yourself, not to rely on your body or your image or your education to define you, but to let your work and let your personality speak for you. Don't rely on those surface level things as an attractive method because people can sense crap. They can smell it. They can sense it from a mile away. They can look through all of your pretty pictures and still not buy because they sense that they're going to be buying from a mannequin and not a real person. They don't promote people who they don't like or they don't feel are relatable or knowledgeable.

Authenticity goes so much further than you can ever imagine in corporate careers and in entrepreneurship because, again, people can sense inauthenticity and it's automatically unattractive. Understand that execution that follows through and dreams that are being lived are radiant and attractive. The law of sowing and reaping is still in effect today. As you sow truth, honesty, clarity, and selflessness, you will begin to reap that in relationships and experiences. What are you attracting?

PART III
REPEAT

Dream, Build, Repeat.

eleven

Activation

Replicate what works and ditch the rest.

It is wise to replicate what works. Stop spending time reinventing the wheel when you could rebuild the same wheel that worked the first time. Since you've walked through these seven steps, you have the tools that you need to follow your dreams unapologetically.

You've realized where you are in your journey.

You've renewed how you see yourself.

You've (likely reluctantly) reviewed your past.

You've finally resurrected that dormant dream.

You've refused to give into negativity.

You've started to run towards the dream.

You've now started to radiate and receive the results of your efforts.

　　　This journey is one that I've walked and will continue walking. It's how I went from feeling frustrated, undervalued, stuck and purposeless to living boldly, doing things that I was previously afraid to do. As a result, I have experienced peace, joy, and success that I only barely dreamed was possible. These keys are not a one-

123

time deal. It's time to find that thing that works for you, build it, and repeat it. This is a living, breathing process and system. Meaning, you can consistently assess and reassess. You should be renewing your mindset. You should be reviewing what happened to you in the past and resurrecting or awakening parts of the dream. Consistently refrain from negativity. Consistently execute the dream and radiate the life of a dream disciple. This process should be repeated over and over and over again, because you'll never run out of growth opportunities. This is a starting point. The idea of having a dream and knowing every single step and every single process until the end of time is not a realistic one. Your dreams will grow, mature, and develop with you.

Six years ago, I was working with my clients on their resumes and career experiences. I realized that I was actually helping applicants get clear and confident in what they bring to the table. So I refined my services to work with young and young-at-heart professionals who felt stagnant and lacked confidence in their lives, faith, careers, and businesses. They realized that they wanted more, but needed support in clarifying their next steps, laying out a strategic plan, and executing their dreams. I assume ten years from now that my approach will be similar, but I'll be growing with my clients. You see, your dreams will grow and develop with you. I've even had to refine to emphasize how my work transcends generations after I consistently received powerful testimonials and feedback from tweens to seniors… at the same events!

As I travel the country speaking as a keynote, on panels, or on podcasts, I've had the privilege to meet so many incredible dreamers. These are dreamers who are at various stages. Some didn't have any idea of their dream or purpose. Some had established brands, careers, and dreams, yet were stuck in a particular place.

Activation

Through coaching others, I've learned that although everyone is unique, there was a reason that each of those clients were attracted to me. Here's an honest moment. I struggled hardcore in the area of doubt and negative thinking regarding business. I started questioning if I had enough experience and expertise to coach these people to their transformation.

A few solid mentors reminded me that if people were coming to me for help and for assistance, then they clearly saw something in me where they could grow, learn, and develop. Let's debunk the myth that you must be a particular age or status in order to do a particular thing. Transformation has less to do with your age, formal education level, and connections. It has more to do with your expertise in a field regardless of how you got that expertise. Eventually, I had to grow and stop discounting my brilliance simply because a particular expertise came naturally to me.

This process began to repeat and I constantly went through the seven steps over and over and over again. I became more and more confident in my abilities and skills. From that one-on-one coaching, I needed to scale my dream to make its impact broader and deeper. This is a lesson for those who are in corporate as well as those who are on the path of entrepreneurship.

In order for you to build an empire from your dream, it has to have a level of scalability. How can you reach more people? How can you reach more of the people who need your assistance? That is a question that you ask in this repeat process. Then the next question that you ask is, *how can you deepen that relationship with the people who are already in your sphere of influence?* How do you deepen that relationship? How do you serve them better? How do you serve them more? How do you serve them differently? How do you continuously grow to meet their needs consistently?

Dream, Build, Repeat.

If you're in that space and you're trying to figure out how you can scale, reach more people, and deepen the relationships with those people, you must master your craft. Having a dream in your mind is not enough. You have to put in the amount of time and effort necessary to achieve mastery. It doesn't mean that you have to know everything right when you first work with someone, but that you are dedicated to mastering your skill. Mastery comes through wisdom, knowledge, industry expertise, and more. It also comes from coaching, from working with someone who's been where you're trying to go, working with someone who can encourage, guide, and keep you accountable as you build and live this dream. Finally, it comes through planning and strategy.

As much as I talk about dreams, I also talk about execution and strategy. A dream left in your head has no value on this earth. Value comes from execution, which is only possible through planning and through strategy. You can duplicate what works and cease doing what doesn't work. Be honest with yourself. How are your conversion rates? How often do people buy from you? Are people clicking on your blog or reading your content? Are people watching your videos? Are people engaged for your talks? Are you getting more clients at the office? Are you being sought after for training? Mastery of your craft comes from consistent review of what's working and what's not working,

Don't do things just because someone told you to. This is your life and your dream. It's nobody else's, so you own it. You own your life. Own your dream, and own your time. Make the most of it. Don't allow people to drive you away from building your dream. Don't allow people's opinions to distract you from living the life that you want to live, but also don't be afraid to reinvent yourself and start this process.

Again, this is a living, breathing guide and manual for you to go from dream to execution. You must dream it. You must build it. You must live it, and you must repeat it. Remember, to live the life of a dream disciple, you must be unapologetic in your honest pursuit of seeing your dream being lived out on earth. It's not the time to be concerned about what everyone else says. It's time to focus on living your life to the fullest. Nobody else can live the life that you were intended to live. Nobody else has the skills that you have. Nobody else has the vision that you have, so fear has to go. Anxiety about not being perfect has to go. Fear of failure has to go. None of those things can live with your dream. None of those things are conducive to where you're going.

There are people who are counting on you. There's a little girl, or a little boy waiting for you to step out and step into your greatness. There is a corporation waiting for you to master that skill. Step out of your comfort zone and step into your zone of genius, regardless of your industry, regardless of your expertise, regardless of your background, there is a place for you. As long as there's breath in your body, as long as you still have your mind, you have something to offer this world.

No matter the size of your dream, it is important. You are important. Your voice is important and it's needed for this time. Stop wasting away and start acting. This is your wake up call. This guide is for you. You are not reading this book by accident. I wrote this book with you in mind. In fact, I was you. I was terrified to step out into the unknown. I was terrified that I would be rejected again. I was terrified that people would remember my failures and my thoughts, my faults. I was terrified to step out into the promised land until one day I realized that fear and my dream could not coexist. I had to realize that in order for me to move forward, to thrive, to radiate, and to live out my dream, I had to kill those negative, toxic thoughts. I had to do something. I had to get clear. I had to step out into the more that was before me.

Repeat. Read this book again. Go back to the chapter that you need at the time. Take notes, journal about your progress, track where you started and where you are ending, and do that over and over again because replicating a good process is profitable, and it is the key to wealth in every area of your life. Invite your friends and your support system on this journey as well. It's never too early and it's never too late.

I had the privilege of speaking at a women's conference for women of faith. I was told by the coordinator of the conference that she was looking for a millennial voice who could speak to the young women who were coming to the conference. I planned a workshop riddled with current slang, references to all of the Internet items, and stories from my young adult life. I was greeted with not a room full of millennials, but a room where the median age was about fifty and the outliers were the three twenty-somethings and the five eighty-somethings.

Initially, I was intimidated by the age gap, but I trusted the message and prayed that it would resonate. At the conclusion of the workshop about dreaming bold dreams, multiple women at or approaching retirement said that they were finally encouraged to dream again. They thought their time had passed and their next step was to relax in retirement. This last story is to remind you that you are called for more than the status quo. It's never too early or too late to start something new. If you ever find yourself in a situation questioning your preparedness, your worthiness, and your message, remember that you were already validated before you entered the room. Your greatness was validated at birth and the path that you're on is for a purpose.

Dream, Build, Repeat.

twelve

Success

You have everything you need within you to succeed.

This is a quote that changed my life. My mentor, Marshawn, said this to me and it shook me. I had this misperception that I was missing the special key to success that was hidden in some course that I hadn't taken yet. I did not realize that I was paralyzed with indecision and inaction. I did not realize that the dreams, gifts, and natural abilities were deposited in me at birth. It was a Dorothy from "The Wizard of Oz" moment, where I realized I had "home" within me all along.

Can you relate? If so, I wrote this book for you. I also wrote this book for the former me. I was that person who was tired of being good, but not good enough. The person who was confused and frustrated by the fact that my life wasn't turning out the way I planned. I constantly questioned why I was going through all of these trials and tribulations. I was exhausted by my career progression. I was dissatisfied with my spiritual journey. It seemed that everybody else was advancing and doing what they were meant to do and I was stuck floundering.

Dream, Build, Repeat.

I wrote this book for you if you're so terrified of failure and people's opinions that you'd rather suffer by not living your dream.

This book was written to give a simple seven-step process that could empower, equip, and encourage you, while giving you a strategy to unleash that dream to the world. It's time out for this idea of doing things *only* for other people. It's time to live the life that you were created to live.

Think about the level of intricacy that was in the process of getting you here into this world. There is a purpose for you. I believe that you were created for such a time as this, but I also believe that it's up to you to start walking down a journey of living out your dream and it's a choice that you have to make. You could choose not to or you could choose to step into the space ordained for you. I hope that this was an awakening for you and that you realize how valuable you are to this planet. You are valuable to this ecosystem and your voice and your expertise are also. Too often we don't realize that even though there are a lot of people in this world, everyone has their own lane. You have your own lane. Even in a saturated market, you can thrive even if it seems like everybody else is doing it. You do it differently. There are countless books in the world, but you bought this one. There are countless teachings on purpose and dreams, but you picked up this one and you read it to the end, which is impressive. That just goes to show you that there is a lane and a message for you, and I want to affirm you in this moment in time.

I want to speak life into your situation. I want to cancel any of those negative thoughts that you've had regarding your worthiness of this journey. I want to cancel any thoughts that you've had that you are not enough or that you don't have enough resources because there is an abundance of resources. You just have to tap in-

132

to them. I want to cancel those thoughts that it's not possible for someone like you to do a particular thing because *it is* possible and maybe the reason that you haven't seen it done is because you are supposed to do it. All of the great inventors of the world have seen a need. They have seen a market that didn't exist yet and they decided to shake it up and do something different. Of course, people didn't want light bulbs because they had fire, so of course there was going to be push back in opposition to the idea of channeling fire another way within a light bulb, but guess what? That was the norm, and that norm was disrupted by another invention. The world is always turning. The seasons are always changing. We're always growing. Remember that just because you don't see it, doesn't mean it's not possible.

I can't stress to you enough that you and your voice are important. I've said that consistently throughout this book because that's what you need to hear. You don't hear that enough. The only consistent voice that is being heard is in the news. The negativity that's happening, how people are marginalized, how there's not enough resources, how there's violence everywhere, how there's all this negativity. Those voices are continuously playing, so I'm coming in to shake things up. I'm coming in to be that voice to encourage you. I'm coming in to be your pocket angel (as my best friend, Lakya affectionately says I am to her). Hopefully you hear my voice loudly and clearly. Anytime negativity comes and you hear my voice that says, "No, no, no. Kick it to the curb. Cast that thought down. Replace it with something fresh." I want to replace all that negativity that you heard from your childhood when you were told that you were not enough and when people placed limiting labels on you. I come against that because what I truly believe is that if you feel restless and a level of urgency then it is truly your time, regardless of your financial status, your marital status, your education level, or your age—this is your season, and because you are here, you have a level of "dream" in you that needs to come into this world right now. Do not despise small beginnings. Do not despise your starting point, because your starting point is all a part of your journey.

Don't focus so much on the finish line that you totally neglect everything that comes from starting. Every part of your journey is a part of your process of growth and development. So now is your time. Now is the time where you realize that you can accelerate your growth through coaching and mentorship. Now is the time where you can accelerate your business by accessing the right plan and the right strategy for your business. Now's the time, so if you're looking to start, get resources in your industry. Get business or career resources in order to accelerate your process because if someone down the street took five years to accomplish something, that doesn't mean that it has to take you five years. It could take you more. It could take you less, so don't place a hard and fast timeline on yourself. Seek out the information you need to know in order to make your life easier. Your dream is valuable. Your voice is valuable. It's time for you to dream it and to build it. It's time for you to repeat it. You have to follow your dreams unapologetically because the world will tell you to be ashamed, but you live an ashamed life.

Good luck, but you don't need it, because you have everything you need inside of you to succeed.
Go get it.
Dream it. Build it. Repeat it.

Thank you!

As a thank you for reading and sharing this book, I have created some training and activations that are exclusive to Dream Disciples! Go to www.CaseySharperson.com click on Book. You'll gain immediate access to activations, accountability, and support. Did I mention that it's free?

Additionally, I invite you to email Hello@CaseySharperson.com to continue the conversation and transformation.

Let's Be Friends!

Tag me on social media and let me know your takeaways, questions, and revelations!
Leave a review on Amazon and Barnes & Noble.

Purchase a copy or a few for your colleagues, friends, and organizations.

Website: www.CaseySharperson.com

Facebook: @CaseyCarea

Instagram: @CaseyCarea

Twitter: @CaseyCarea

YouTube: Casey Sharperson

Email: Hello@CaseySharperson.com

Podcast: Dream Build Repeat with Casey Sharperson

Request Me to Speak

Have a retreat, conference, podcast or corporate gathering where you need a dynamic speaker or trainer? Head over to www.CaseySharperson.com to submit a request.

About The Author

Casey Sharperson, known as The Confidence Cultivator™, is a speaker, podcaster, business and brand strategist to women (and a few smart men) desiring clarity and strategy to increase their income and influence. With a background in corporate training, professional development, and digital marketing, she is passionate to see others live out their dreams, profitably. Her proprietary systems and the Dream Disciple Academy have become the premiere blueprint for her clients to execute their dreams and stand out in a cluttered marketplace. Named DMV's Top 30 under 30, she is committed to elevating her clients to reach their biggest dreams with clear, concise actionable plans.

As the creator and host of the Dream, Build, Repeat podcast, Casey provides personal insight, encouragement, and inspiration for the dreamer on the go. She interviews people who are defying the odds and changing their influence one day at a time. Ultimately she shows what it looks like to live a life committed to purpose, passion, and impact.

Casey graduated with honors from Claflin University, as a member of The Alice Carson Tisdale Honors College, where she was named Who's Who in American Colleges & Universities and earned national recognition by being awarded the Cultured Pearls Leadership Award, which was presented at Alpha Kappa Alpha Sorority Incorporated's Boule in 2012. As a senior in college, she authored L.E.A.P: A Comprehensive Tool to Market Study Abroad to Minorities, serving as a catalyst for her entrepreneurial work. A few of Casey's clients include: The Advisory Board Company, Education Advisory Board, Married & Young, Miller Media Group, Claflin University, More Than Cheer, Fearless Conference, South Carolina State University, Power Up Women's Conference, Build Your Own Brand Society, Camp Read-A-Rama (Clemson University), Clemson Elementary School, and Freeway Church.